BRAIN
IN
BALANCE

BRAIN
IN
BALANCE

UNDERSTANDING THE GENETICS AND NEUROCHEMISTRY BEHIND ADDICTION AND SOBRIETY

Fredrick Von Stieff, M.D.

First Edition

Canyon Hill Publishing   San Francisco, California

This edition was prepared for publishing by
Ghost River Images
5350 East Fourth Street
Tucson, Arizona 85711
www.ghostriverimages.com

Cover design by Chen Design

ISBN 978-1475045673

Library of Congress Control Number: 2011938500

Printed in the United States of America

March, 2012

Contents

About the Author

Dr. Von Stieff is a recognized expert in the field of chemical dependency treatment. He is a board-certified addictionologist who has successfully detoxified over 20,000 patients in hospital-based programs. He has worked as the Medical Director for three different chemical dependency programs over the course of twenty years and is certified by the American Board of Addiction Medicine, the American Society of Addiction Medicine, and the California Society of Addiction Medicine. He is currently the Chief Medical Review Officer for the State of California and a legal expert in substance abuse, carrying additional titles in that field.

He comes from humble beginnings in central Nevada and started his higher education at the University of Nevada. He graduated from the University of California Irvine Medical School and then completed a family practice residency at the University of California Davis. He then began working at hospitals in the East Bay of San Francisco, where he not only worked in chemical dependency, but also spent time working as an assistant in both vascular surgery and brain surgery. It was during that time of striving to understand the brain better and working in a chemical dependency program, that he began to develop many new, innovative ideas about detoxification and treatment.

At first Dr. Von Stieff went through a phase of feeling distrust, annoyance, and even anger towards addicts and alcoholics, but he soon realized there was more behind their addiction than just a series of bad life choices. Something else was going on within their brains that provided a further explanation for their actions. After working with these addicted individuals that he once viewed as disgraceful, he found that they actually had a number of reputable qualities such as intelligence, charm, and humor. So what was the difference between them and the rest of society? They just had an affliction – its source being neurochemical, which needed special treatment. They required innovative ways to keep them out of harm's way and prevent them from losing their lives due to the consequences of some state of mind not in congruence with their character.

Thus Dr. Von Stieff dedicated years to studying the brain's neurochemicals with the goal of trying to fit a vast puzzle of information about the brain into a recognizable picture that could be used to help these patients. He learned how to utilize mechanisms contained in the workings of the brain, and now with this information, he provides the most cutting-edge and effective treatment for his patients, with lasting results and minimal relapses. After helping thousands of patients each year and educating other medical professionals on the latest methods of focusing on neurochemical balances throughout treatment, Dr. Von Stieff could no longer deny the need to publish a book. In addition to establishing that there are rules that the brain adheres to, it is Dr. Von Stieff's desire to assist all to understand the brain and its inclinations better and to help dissolve the mystery behind addiction and successful treatment.

His passion lies in providing the best service to his patients by continually discovering and refining the most advanced techniques, along with designing medication regimens to make their detoxification as comfortable, quick, and safe as possible. He is driven by his fascination with the brain and his curiosity to learn how it works under different circumstances. As an avid researcher, he has spent years analyzing the brain, trying to assemble a comprehensive and concise explanation for the mechanisms of this dynamic organ. By sharing this knowledge of the brain in practice, he has helped patients and their families to understand how they can succeed in becoming and remaining sober.

Dr. Von Stieff has received many awards for his achievements. He was ranked in the top one percent of doctors in California when *San Francisco Magazine* designated him as being a "Top Doc." Seventeen thousand doctors and nurses voted him into that position. Throughout his career of thousands of detoxifications, none of his patients have ever passed away, had a code blue, nor had a grand mal seizure. The Joint Chiefs of Hospital Accreditation recently labeled his work and its success rate as "miraculous." The examiner making that statement indicated that that was the first time he had ever said that about a physician, his work, and the accomplishments of the unit he directs. Dr. Von Stieff has also won awards in the chemical dependency field locally and has been featured on television to promulgate his ideas on chemical dependency.

When he is not attempting to save the world one person at a time or advancing the field of detoxification, he enjoys working on his ranch with his horses and goats, as well as spending time with his wife and three grown children.

Preface

In view of the millions who suffer from addiction problems and neurochemical imbalances, it became imperative to me that a book be written that could both reach the novice and enlighten the professional on the latest discoveries in this area of science. Shedding light on the brain and its neurochemicals, this book identifies the source of addiction and thereby reveals the most recent, cutting-edge, and effective methods and techniques in treatment.

I am a board-certified addictionologist at a hospital-based institution with extensive experience in detoxification. Following the lectures on the chemicals of the brain that I have delivered to countless physicians, nurses, and staff of various hospitals throughout the San Francisco Bay Area, I have received numerous questions about the lectures' contents. Audiences consistently ask where they can get more information about the rules of the brain described in the lecture and the brain's neurochemicals, also referred to as neurotransmitters. (The terms *neurochemical* and *neurotransmitter* are used interchangeably throughout the book.) Up until now, I have only been able to offer an incomplete list of sources and books that fail to provide any kind of concise understanding. Many have recommended that I put my thoughts and knowledge down on paper – creating a book on how I perceive the brain's functions in a clinical manner and how I orchestrate the neurotransmitters in daily practice.

It is rare to find someone with a solid grasp on the global functioning aspect of the brain – the basic interrelationships among its neurochemicals that determine how we function on a higher level. More often than not, physicians, family therapists, and other healthcare professionals do not understand how the patients' neurochemicals are being affected by both the detoxification and the medications being administered to ease the symptoms associated with that process. The purpose of this book is to fill that void of understanding because people's lives, depression, psychological conditioning, and successful detoxification are dependent upon these principles.

After years of studying the brain and reading everything I could get my hands on about neurotransmitters and why the brain had rules that it followed, I began to think that it was more than I could possibly comprehend. There are excellent books on neurotransmitters, but few on more of a global view and brain rules of their executive functions. One can get lost in all the information available on chemical reactions and yet be unable to apply the knowledge. However, I kept at it and continued applying what I was learning to my clinical practice. My efforts to take the puzzle pieces of each of the never-ending new discoveries in neuroscience and integrate them into one comprehensive understanding were challenging to say the least, but because of it, I have reaped excellent results. Eighty-five percent of our patients are still sober one year after completing our program, and we have never turned down anyone from entering the facility. Our success is not based on chance; we get such astounding results because we address patients' neurochemical imbalances, educate them, and treat their imbalances along with any other psychiatric disorders they may have.

The information found in this book is filling a major gap of knowledge that the health care system has been missing for years.

We have taken the typical book about neurotransmitters to a new level where you will learn rules that the brain works by, along with methods that are explained in a way that finally makes the use of neurotransmitters applicable in practice. That is the difference between this and other books. It would be an injustice for this information to be withheld from either medical professionals or the public. This book will help alcoholics and addicts understand why they feel the way they do, and this knowledge will prove to be a source of power for them. The medical professionals who read this book will be better equipped to provide relief to their patients from the pains of addiction. Thus those who, due to heredity, have a predisposition towards these afflictions can have a healthy, productive life. Meanwhile, we will continue to find new ways to grow in our knowledge and share it with other institutions so they too can have a share in this kind of success.

Acknowledgments

The most informative and effective books are born of both personal experience and a vast array of external sources and inspirations. For such a book as this, any list of acknowledgements fit within the confines of one page would fail to convey all the thanks that are owed to those who helped make it possible. There are too many individuals, Pubmed.com articles, books, and other published works to mention that have contributed to this multi-faceted topic of neurochemistry. First of all, I want to thank my wife Sherry and my children, Jim, Fred Jr. and Kristi, for all of their sacrifices. I would also like to give a special thanks to the following people, whose support helped breathe life into this book: Katie Schuh Juarez, for her vast work in editing and planning; the late Rolph Sommerhaug, M.D., who had faith in my ICU management cases; Ethel Roehl, R.N., for her daily support in treating difficult cases using this method along with other ICU nurses for their faith in this methodology; research chemist Dr. Rick Carpenter, for applications; hospital pharmacist Kevin Lane, who for years has discussed and shared with me the latest research on drugs; medical student Kristi Carpenter, for fluency and clarity; the National Institute of Drug Abuse, for their publications; the American Society of Addiction Medicine; the California Society of Addiction Medicine; the psychiatrists, addictionologists, and pain management specialists throughout the San Francisco Bay Area who continue to refer patients; Elizabeth Zunino, for her graphics; Chen Design for their cover design; Ghost River Images, for their expertise in publishing; and psychiatrists Dr. O.B. Towery, Dr. Mel McGraw, Dr. Brad Gould, and others who have taught me so much. Finally, I would like to thank all the nurses and doctors at hospitals throughout the Bay Area who have encouraged me to write this book, along with writer Anne Courtney for encouraging me to write the first paragraph.

Introduction

The brain, like the universe or any living organism, exists not in a static state, but rather in a state of dynamic equilibrium. Science is based on observation and experimentation, out of which theories and eventually laws are developed to explain natural phenomena and how they function. With this book, I have attempted to define how essential neurotransmitters work within the structure of the brain, influencing how it functions. As an addictionologist, doing research and working with patients, I have been afforded the opportunity to extract the rules by which the brain behaves. It is by examining these rules, that we are given the clues necessary to effectively treat a brain suffering from an imbalance or going through the process of detoxification.

The rules outlined within the pages of this book explain both how the brain works and how to treat a brain suffering from withdrawal. The rules can be found at the end of every chapter under the subheading *Brain Rules*. These rules are contrived from the author's observations and research, and are unique to this text. Case studies are featured at the end of the book to demonstrate how healthcare professionals can apply these rules in daily practice. Accompanying some of those case studies, there are samples of how to view patients' neurotransmitters when diagnosing and treating their chemical imbalances using the *neurotransmitter diagram* that I have developed. The section entitled, *How to Visualize Patients' Neurotransmitter Systems* explains the different ways to use these neurotransmitter diagrams. In addition, there is a drug index in the back that lists some medications and drugs, and summarizes which neurotransmitters they affect and how they do so.

This is a new and exciting approach to neurochemistry. Instead of looking at the brain globally, we have been buried in a finite science of looking at the micro sciences of each nerve; thus, people have not been able to see the forest for the trees. Often the effects of drugs on the neurotransmitter systems are mentioned, but no one ever brings up the fact that these systems communicate and are dependent on one another. Nor has it been discussed that when people use illicit drugs or medications that affect one system, inevitably the other systems that are connected will adjust themselves in some reactionary balance to the change. The neurotransmitter systems are dynamic, and to our folly, we have been so wrapped up in details, that we have missed the big picture.

On the other hand, taking a step back to look at and understand the global system within the brain means that this book is an oversimplification of the neurotransmitter systems. Other information and literature on neurotransmitters are tremendously vast, complicated, and difficult to learn. Because the brain is such a dynamic and complex piece of work with plenty of research and discoveries being made on it every day from various sources, learning neurochemistry can be like trying to put a thousand-piece puzzle together, with none of the pieces fitting together exactly right.

Usually the most effective way to build a puzzle is to start on the borders and then work your way towards the center. However, because of the way that research has become available to us, it has not been possible to piece the puzzle of neurotransmitters together this way. By having us start our studies with the very basic structure of the synapse and then try to comprehend what the rest of the world around it is like, popular science has complicated the way we understand the brain. On the contrary, what I am offering readers is a chance to start at the borders as it were, by looking at the global function of the neurotransmitters and their systems within the brain and then from that vantage point, look inward at what is happening, forming rules as we go.

Though my methods of explanation will lead to a much clearer and comprehensive understanding of how the brain functions (especially in reaction to medications and illicit drugs), there are caveats to this approach. One *must* understand that there is more complexity underneath the superficial look that we are about to address in this book. There is a lot of research going on and also a significant amount of complexity when it comes to interactions that are beyond the scope of this book. For instance there is optimal dosing of anti-psychotics, drug interactions, and other body functions that all affect the neurotransmitter systems. What this book is however, is an introduction to a new conceptual approach to the study of the brain.

Disclaimer

This book was written to disseminate information on the rules of the brain, the complex interactions of the brain and its neurochemical balances. The concepts found within this book, although based on research and experience, are interpreted by its author. Though they have been extensively used in his methodology of treatment, there may be discrepancies in scientific research and findings as well as the content of this book. The author of this book, its supporters that originated it, and its publisher are not responsible for the outcome of a patient if the methods discussed herein are used. This book is sold with the understanding that neither the publisher nor the author is rendering medical advice or any other professional services such as the interpretation or analysis of the human brain that might lead to treatment or any other recommendations including but not exclusive to the changing or adjustment of medications or the purchasing of any medications to treat, analyze, withhold, or combine them in any manner.

Reading this book, though it will inform the reader on the latest methods in treatment, will not make the reader a certified detoxification specialist nor will it make the reader an authority on brain analysis. Individuals should never alter their medication regimen without the advice and supervision of a certified medical professional. Knowledge in the field of neurochemistry and detoxification is always increasing and everyone's brain chemistry is unique to each individual, therefore there is no absolute guarantee of success in any method of treatment.

No endorsements of any medications are made by either the author, the publisher, or anyone else involved in the creation of this book. The author does not endorse any pharmaceutical products nor the companies that produce them. The author did not and does not receive any compensation from any pharmaceutical company for any statement within this book. Any statement, whether positive or negative, made in this book about any commercial product is the author's personal view and may be right or wrong and should be considered so; they should be received by the reader as an individual's opinions, not facts.

The author and all those involved in the production of this book are in no way connected or associated with Brain Balance Centers. This book is one of many titles on the subject of the brain's balance and to the publishing date, has no competitive aspect or endorsement of any entity, book, or business associated with Brain Balance concepts.

This book recommends strict privacy of medical and psychiatric information according to the law. Any and all case studies included or alluded to throughout the book are produced from generalities of chemical dependency. It is by chance and not by purpose if similarities are found between an individual in a case and the reader. There is no intent to identify or harm anyone with the narrative; its purpose is to educate.

Every effort has been made to supply the reader with accurate information and an accurate interpretation of research, but there may exist mistakes both in content and typography. We are in the infancy of this field of brain chemical treatment, and the knowledge that we do have, has a high degree of variability. Therefore this book should be interpreted only as a general guide to neurochemistry and detoxification information, and consultation with a Board Certified Physician for confirmation of the contents of this book must be sought before any action on the reader's part is taken. The information in this book is not a substitute for routine medical care, and if used, should be used solely in conjunction with the medical care and supervision of a physician. Any questions that arise should be directed to your health care provider. Prior to using any of the techniques or information contained within this book, it is essential to consult with one's physician. It is the understanding of the author that the reader will perform his or her own research to confirm the contents of this manuscript. This manuscript is written to both inform and entertain.

The purpose of this book is to educate both medical professionals and neophytes. Dr. Von Stieff and all associated with the production of this book will not be held accountable for the use and interpretation of the contents of this book with regards to treatment or any other material covered in this book. The author and all those involved in the production of this book shall have neither liability nor responsibility to any person, business, institution or any other entity with respect to any loss or damage caused, or alleged to have been caused, directly or indirectly, by the information contained or interpreted in this book, neither can they be held liable for any errors, inaccuracies, or omissions.

If you do not agree to the terms within this disclaimer or you do not desire to be bound by the above, you may return this book for a full refund.

"The functions of the brain are so foreseeable that the science of chemical dependency is just as predictable as the science of cardiology."

Chapter I

The Brain –
A Complex, yet Predictable Organ

One hundred billion neurons make up the amazing brain. Do not underestimate the dynamic activity that goes on in and amongst these special cells. They are not isolated entities; rather they are all connected in one way or another, with joined hands so to speak. Among them, they have different languages and func tions. Just as the world is made up of many nations, the brain is divided into functional states called *neurotransmitter systems*. Each of these systems of neurons communicates using its own language and functions first independently and then as part of a network of systems, much like a sovereign nation functions separately yet is influenced by the other nations of the world. In both situations there is interdependence and imbalances. Scientists have studied the neurotransmitter systems extensively and published findings that are very complex, detail-oriented, and complicated, even for professionals. It is not really necessary to know all those complex little details to understand the beauty of how the brain and its neurotransmitters work.[1]

The predictability and consistency of the work performed by the brain demands that rules be ascribed to the science of neurochemistry and detoxification; that is what this book is all about. This book first delves into the basics of neurotransmitters. The analysis and treatment process of detoxification will be discussed, as well as how different medications affect each of the neurotransmitter systems systematically. The fun really starts as you are transformed into a pro at brain rules and methods of neurotransmitter analysis. So enjoy your travels into the fascinating world that science has made inconceivable until now.

Rules for the Brain???

It is true! The brain functions according to a set of rules, and because I work in conjunction with those rules every day, I have taken on the task of mapping out those rules for the world to see, clearing up some of the ambiguity of what goes on within our skulls. The brain and its neurotransmitters actually run according to a set of principles, making them act in a very predictable fashion. In fact, the functions of the brain are so foreseeable that the science of chemical dependency is just as predictable as the science of cardiology.

Just as a cardiologist is able to look at a patient's symptoms and determine which disease or malady his or her heart is suffering from, a trained chemical dependency specialist is capable of analyzing a patient's symptoms and determining what neurochemical imbalance exists in the brain of that patient. The heart, a mechanical organ, functions in a very predictable manner, which allows the cardiologist to visualize the contending disease and then select one of various medications to improve the cardio dynamics of the diseased heart. The outcome that follows is usually quite predictable. So too, when

---

1 The terms *neurotransmitter(s)* and *neurochemical(s)* are used interchangeably throughout the book.

an addictionologist or physician analyzes a brain's neurochemical imbalance correctly, the outcome of their treatment is equally as predictable. He or she can use various medications to correct the imbalance of neurotransmitters with the same likelihood of success in response to the medications that cardiologists experience when treating their patients.

On the other hand, there are definitely aspects of the brain that make it a bit more complex to work with. For instance, the brain is not static in function; on the contrary, it is always changing – up-regulating or down-regulating, trying to reach a balance of its neurotransmitters.[2] It exists in a state of dynamic equilibrium and therefore automatically seeks its own natural balance. Unfortunately, its methods of doing so often wreak havoc on the body. To try to figure out where the brain is on its way to neurochemical satisfaction and final balance is challenging to say the least. The brain is programmed to do the work that it needs to do so that it can function in a way that it perceives as normal. One can clinically observe this phenomenon in the detoxifying brains of alcoholics, opiate addicts, and other drug-addicted patients. Where that regulation is centered is uncertain, but my guess is that it is centered in the mid forebrain bundle. Why it happens is obvious – the brain is out of balance and seeks normality, and dealing with that process is what withdrawal and detoxification is all about.

For Every Action, There is a Reaction

The brain and its neurotransmitter systems, like any other system in the universe, function according to rules of balance and interaction. The entire universe is characterized by things that are in balance, from the solar system of planets to the global execu-

---

2 When used in this book, the term *up-regulate* refers to the brain's naturally occurring attempt at returning to its innate neurochemical balance. Detailed explanations of what occurs during both up-regulation and down-regulation will be covered in chapter 5.

tive financial system; balance is the order that makes things work. Einstein knew that fact with his laws of physics, as did Carl Sagan with the study of astrophysics. Stephen Hawking's research has demonstrated that the universe works according to a very unique balance of planetary physics and forces. If there is a disruption, such as a giant asteroid hitting one of the planets, an adjustment occurs so that all the forces of gravitation will equalize after the impact.

Likewise, the brain's neurotransmitter systems can also be disturbed by an impact from external forces such as illicit drugs and alcohol. Prescription medications also have a significant influence on these systems. In addition, the brain's neurochemical balance is challenged daily by other hormonal and environmental factors. The extent of the disturbance and repercussions caused by the impact depends upon the frequency of occurrence and the amount of force connected with each impact, as well as how the system reacts to that particular type of impact. Depending on the above-mentioned factors and the individual being affected, the neurotransmitter systems may be steadfast or they may change with little resistance. The point is, the brain reacts to the outside forces of alcohol and drugs, illicit or prescribed, and the neurochemical systems react by forming a new balance. When the forces of drug abuse are terminated, the systems seek their natural balance, and that's when we have issues of withdrawal to contend with.

I currently work at a twelve-bed detoxification unit, where I have jokingly described myself as a fry cook with an eight-foot long grill. This grill concept occurred to me as a result of spending my early years alongside my father, a chef on the Las Vegas strip. It may sound impersonal, but it is the best way to describe how these brains are constantly up-regulating, "jumping" about like cold meat hitting a hot grill, trying to find their natural balance by going through complex chemical changes. Then there are those brains that become so tremulous that they jump off the grill. Nevertheless, each brain going through withdrawal knows how to up-regulate (or cook so to speak) until they reach their natural balance, except for brain number seven. Brain number seven does not know how to find its balance; it is a methamphetamine brain. Its regulatory system has been affected by the drug itself, making it unable to up-regulate correctly. But the brains do not do *all* the work; the doctors and nurses see to it that the right amounts of medicinal spices are added at the right time. These medications are used to insure that the brains' neurochemicals get to their proper balance with minimal complications and no seizures.

Meanwhile, as the brain is searching for its proper point of balance, the body reflects what is happening in the brain. Medical students often miss this fact because they are not taught to refine their ability of observation. Professors teach them to learn from instruction. What they really need to do is *see* or observe their patients closely and deduce what is actually occurring from those observations.

"Open your eyes and look," I tell the new students who come to learn in the hospital setting. "Do not speak. Take more than a minute and *really* look at the patient that you are caring for and ask yourself, 'What do I see?' Look at their eyes. Where are they focused?"

People on drugs do not even look into their own baby's eyes, let alone the eyes of the people caring for them. Their eyes rove about without purpose, much like their brain in its randomized search for balance. Facial expressions are varied and not in tune with the content of their speech. There are disturbing inconsistencies. The movement of their hands and legs may also lack purpose, and often the items in their room will be in as much disarray as their state of mind. When we know a family member is behaving out of the norm, we intuitively sense that change; however, we rarely stop to observe the fine details necessary to grasp a clear understanding of how it is the brain is making those actions available for us to read.

After years of studying neurotransmitters and working in the field of detoxification, I realized that this area of science could be made so much easier to understand and work with, simply by focusing on the global functions of the neurotransmitter systems. In spite of this new understanding, there are still a lot of complications that occur in the process of detoxification. At times, it can feel like a juggling act when detoxifying patients. So many things can go wrong. For instance, the brain can start going too fast because of high agitating glutamate levels, but with the right medications, this can be balanced out. I am pleased to say that we have not had a grand mal seizure in over ten thousand detoxifications because of the medications we use to oppose glutamate. In addition, the liver can go into hyper drive within the peak of the detoxification, burning up all the medications that are administered to try to slow the body and brain down. (These and other complications will be discussed further in future chapters.) Furthermore, we are often dealing with a multitude of other medical problems in addition to withdrawal. Symptoms of various cardiac, hypertension problems, diabetes, history of previous seizures or hepatic failure will suddenly be magnified as one progresses through the detoxification and may need daily or even hourly attention.

Why You Need to Know the Basics

In order to deal with these kinds of situations and prescribe the correct drug, it is imperative to be familiar with eight of the neurotransmitter systems (serotonin, dopamine, gamma-aminobutyric acid (GABA), glutamate, opiate, noradrenergic, endocannabinoid, and acetylcholine). I have spent over thirty years working as a physician in general practice, at hospitals, and also in addiction medicine. Most physicians are greatly influenced by the pharmaceutical industry when it comes to the understanding of neurochemicals and the prescription of psychiatric drugs and deciding which medications they will prescribe for conditions like depression. This is highly unfortunate because that influence is based upon what he or she has learned from the marketing of these various neurochemical drug companies.

When a drug representative comes into the office to market a medication to the physician, the representative will discuss important issues such as the drug's effectiveness for depression and other mood disorders, but they will rarely discuss which neurotransmitters will be affected. When I am being introduced to a new medicine, I make a practice of asking the drug representative which neurotransmitters the product affects as well as how drastically they are affected. I also inquire whether the drug is an agonist (stimulant) or an antagonist (inhibitor) to those neuroreceptors. Sometimes the representatives will have the answers, but often they are left somewhat dumbfounded and tell me they will have to get back to me later with those answers from the research department of their drug companies.

At times just finding out what the drug does and how effective it is, is enough to determine which neurotransmitters are involved and what effect the drug will have on those systems. Once one understands the eight neurotransmitter systems, one can almost tell immediately what the drug is going to be used for. For instance, dopamine and noradrenaline typically are used to treat bipolar disorder. GABA drugs are naturally sedating, while glutamate is more for agitation and memory. There are a lot of serotonin drugs, some of which are effective in treating alcoholism and other drug addiction problems. Learning the basic format of the neurochemicals gives insight and allows one to make good judgment as to what will or will not be effective.

Listening to a drug representative and trying to make a decision about which drug to prescribe can be somewhat of a conflict of interest, thus it behooves one to know the basics of neurochemistry. If a doctor understands the neurochemical imbalance of a patient, he or she can pick the appropriate drug for the patient's particular condition. Whether that patient's imbalance or deficiency is genetic or simply the result of some illicit drug abuse, with the right tools of knowledge, an appropriate medication can be chosen by the medical professional.

If the medical professional relies solely on the information provided by the drug representative, without this insight and basic understanding of neurochemistry, he or she can actually make the patient worse. I have seen this situation happen over and over again with patients who have general anxiety or ADHD. For example, after hearing a patient complain of depression, anxiety, and insomnia, a physician has to pick a medicine that will work for all three problems. The physician proceeds to try to find the right drug to solve the patient's problems. Typically the choice is one that suddenly comes to mind without a lot of analysis, but rather through intuitive factors. That's when the doctor says "OK, I have something for you to try!" That intuition comes from using the drug by trial and error in many prior patients, so patients essentially get pigeonholed into categories mentally for different drug types that seem to work.

The methodology described in this book is more introspective and scientific. Sure, a Harvard Psychiatrist with thirty years of experience of prescribing antidepressant medications to patients and seeing the results is able to pigeonhole people into different categories quite successfully. Personally, however, in deciding which medication will and will not work, I need more methodology behind my decisions than my intuition gives me. Things can get really complicated whenever there are numerous factors you have to contend with such as people's genetic predispositions, chemical dependency, stress problems, and allergies to medications. This book provides that needed understanding on the basics of those neurochemicals, how to analyze a patient, and how to prescribe a medication that precisely fits the needs of the patient.

It usually takes about one or two times to pick the most effective drug. By *effective*, I mean that the patient feels better than they have in a long time. In the case of drug or alcohol abusers, having effective results means they have not relapsed because the drug has suppressed the cravings and caused the patients to experience less anxiety and a sense of well-being that they have not experienced for a long time. That is what I call *effective*. Attaining those kinds of results is contingent upon gaining that fundamental understanding of the basic principles and concepts of neurochemistry. How one can determine if and which neurochemical deficiency their patient has, how to analyze it, and how to properly treat each deficiency will be discussed throughout this book.

Why Use this System

The brain, the most advanced executive structure known to man, has long been the focus of inquiring minds throughout the world. Reading this book about the works of the brain and the interrelationships among eight of its neurotransmitter systems will provide many answers to the uncertainty of chemical dependency and its infamous problems. Among other things, it will make determining neurochemical balances easier. The information within these chapters will clear up what science literature has thus far made vague and overly complex.

After devoting years to studying the complexities involved with the brain and the relationships among its neurotransmitters, it became apparent there must be a less complicated way of handling these systems. This new understanding sheds light on why people use drugs and alcohol and how underlying psychiatric conditions outlined in the **Diagnostic and Statistical Manual** (DSM-IV) are related. Using the system laid out in the pages of this book has benefits that far out-weigh the risks. Certainly all of us, whether we are parents, physicians, or treatment specialists, need to find a method and a treatment that will produce more benefits than harm; therefore, we must go for probabilities.

Where there is uncertainty, more information is needed. How does one gather data about how the brain works? When treating a patient, one must take the following factors into consideration: genetics, past drug use, current addictions, past medications, cravings, and present disposition. When the medical staff has access to all these facts, the treatment success rate is higher because there is sufficient information to begin the process of determining the imbalance at hand and which medications are best at eliminating cravings and symptoms of withdrawal. As you will see in the following chapter, there is no other methodology in treatment that has reaped such positive results.

Brain Rules

Rule #1: The brain and its neurochemical systems function in a very predictable manner.

Rule #2: Significant drug use alters the brain's neurochemical balance.

Rule #3: No matter what illicit or prescription drugs are taken or discontinued, the brain's neurochemical systems will always attempt to return to their genetically-set levels.

"Every good and useful method starts out as a theory. It is only when we venture into precarious territory that we can make advancement and science can forge ahead."

Chapter 2

Addressing Neurochemical Balances: Validity of this Method

Just the other day when conferring with a psychiatrist regarding a mutual patient, he questioned whether or not the patient needed to be in detoxification. I gave him the history of the patient, explaining that it was her second day of detoxification from alcohol and opiates and that she was very depressed and crying. When I started discussing the patient's high blood pressure, rapid heart rate, depression, and genetic history, the psychiatrist stopped me and said that he wasn't interested in all of that. He was only concerned about her vital signs, whether or not she was in withdrawal, and how much Ativan was given.

A Common Methodological Blunder

I tried to explain that there were other pertinent factors involved, like neurotransmitter imbalances and possible genetic abnormalities that needed to be addressed. The psychiatrist stated that

that was all theoretical and not based on any scientific knowledge. He proceeded to say that we should not look at those neurochemical problems because it had *nothing* to do with this patient. A long discussion ensued, and it became quite evident that the psychiatrist was not at all interested in the neurotransmitter systems of the brain, nor in what they do.

His method, like many other people in his field, is to make a diagnosis by intuition. They speak to their patients and observe them, assessing their emotional stability, and then they take an educated guess as to which antidepressant, anti-psychotic, or atypical psychotic medication they should prescribe. They base their decisions on past cases, where they gain a feel for the response of the different medications. It is of no concern to them whether or not that patient had a neurochemical deficiency to begin with, nor do they consider how their prescribed medications affect the patient's neurotransmitter systems. They merely intuitively prescribe and watch the results by having the patient come back for a follow-up appointment.

Of course not all psychiatrists are so close minded to all the present advancements that are being made within their field. There are a lot of open-minded psychiatrists who keep up to date with all the latest advances and discoveries surrounding neurotransmitters. They consider it part of their duty in providing optimal treatment for their patients. These kinds of inquisitive and well-educated psychiatrists are interested in the mechanisms of neurotransmitters and how they are affected by medications, as well as methods that will help them and their patients.

Evaluation and Success

Clearly, however, this particular psychiatrist had dismissed the tracking of neurotransmitter balances during the detoxification process as completely theoretical with no scientific basis at all. Unfortunately he had closed his mind to the kind of scientific advancement that has made our detoxification unit such an amazing success.

As the conversation came to a conclusion, I sat there for a while pondering over the twenty thousand people whom we had detoxified. I thought about the most difficult cases of detoxification – the patients in the intensive care unit who were intubated with severe agitation, the people who nobody else could get off the ventilator. I thought about the many bipolar patients who required detoxification from opiates and the alcoholics who carried with them many other symptoms including depression, genetic alcoholism, and cross-addiction. I thought of all these diverse cases and how if it were not for my knowledge of the eight neurotransmitter systems, I would not have been able to successfully detoxify these ailing individuals.

One of the biggest insurance companies recently asked how we manage to help patients recover so quickly, as well as maintain a higher success rate than other facilities. They actually requested to see the facility for themselves. There is no mystery about it. This unmatched success is due to our program and the staff's understanding of the brain rules and the relevance of patients' neurotransmitter balances and their taking the time to make an integrated assessment of each individual in a methodical manner and then responding accordingly. This is what we are teaching you how to do in this book.

Relapse: The Measure of Achievement

Throughout the chemical dependency industry, it is well known that people who go through treatment programs have a high risk of relapse. Within the first year, roughly 50 percent of patients who complete a detoxification program will eventually relapse.

The key to relapse prevention is to go beyond the superficial level of treatment and actually address the underlying cravings and neurochemical imbalances head-on. Simply put, cravings are the result of an imbalance of neurotransmitters. Therefore the most logical way to prevent alcoholics and other drug-addicted people from having a relapse is to go straight to the root of the problem and treat the neurochemical imbalances that are the cause of the cravings. The first step to treating people effectively is to address and analyze the patient's neurochemical balance. One must note the changes that the detoxification process makes to their existing (most-likely abnormal) neurochemical balances. Then one must administer the appropriate neurotransmitter drugs, first to make the detoxification progress as smoothly as possible, and then afterwards to prevent cravings. If we work with the cravings and understand what neurotransmitters are lacking or out of balance, we can surely increase these patients' ability to have consistent sobriety within the years to come. Our 85 percent sobriety rate is proof thereof. Having a program that goes beyond the initial detoxification with things like a 28-day program and intensive care relapse programs, is also necessary to be most effective.

My fellow workers and I have found that following the methodology of addressing neurochemical imbalances has reaped excellent results. I am very happy with our statistics and with the treatment protocols that have been given. We have had no grand mal seizure activity in over fifteen thousand detoxifications, nor have we had any cardiac arrests or any other major complications. This is because of our keen eye and assessment of patients' neurotransmitters, in addition to close consideration of the other physical problems that they have. (Yes, some seizures are caused by neurochemical imbalances.) Our patients' 85 percent sobriety rate after one year of completing the program includes the 7,000 visits per year and the 1,000 inpatient detoxifications. It should be noted that where I work, we accept and treat all people, regardless of the severity of their condition. What makes the minimal amount of relapses possible is our method of not only addressing and treating the patients' neurochemical imbalances, but also addressing and treating any possible psychiatric disorders they might have. Psychiatric disorders and chemical imbalances are both closely tied to the eight neurotransmitter systems.

No Longer Just a Theory

That long period of analysis and self-examination after the conversation with that psychiatrist really hit home. Using the neurochemical methodology to treat chemical dependency and psychiatric patients has proven quite successful. The fact is, when the chips are down and no one else can help a patient with extreme circumstances – like one patient who had a post bypass graft and severe agitation, among other additional complications – one has to use the best scientific methodology science has to offer. If the medical staff doesn't have any scientific basis or methodology for the care of their patients, the complications and risks are exceedingly high. Though it may take a few tries to accurately pin-point what exactly the imbalance is, using the neurochemical schematics, the neurochemical formulation, and the treatment protocols described in this book works virtually every time. Without these techniques, I do not believe that anyone else could have gotten that above-mentioned patient off the ventilator within seventy-two hours. These progressive and revolutionary methods consistently make what seems to be impossible, possible.

It seems the study of the neurochemical systems of the brain is becoming more wide spread. Addictionologists and research departments in institutions such as Stanford, University of California Berkeley and Davis are all paying more attention to the study of brain chemicals and how they work. Keeping up with their findings published in scientific medical literature, I have been able to combine their research with my experience in the ICU and have thus gained deep insight into the application of neurotransmitter systems. I have observed how each neurotransmitter system is related to one another and how each system is affected by various medications. While doing this, I have pieced together the various neurochemical reactions into a simplified arrangement, which we will teach you.

The methodology behind using these neurotransmitter systems in treatment has consistently worked for me in the detoxification unit, with post detoxification patients, and especially in the most complicated of situations. No other existing method of treatment works this quickly and effectively. Without this method and the knowledge I have about the neurotransmitter systems, I would be lost. I quite frankly could not do the work that I do today without using this method. With every passing day and in every case that I use it, the method validates itself. This is the reason I am promoting it and writing about the eight basic neurotransmitter systems that are so vital to determining our quality of life. Knowledge of these systems ought to be spread so that medical professionals can more effectively treat their patients.

People with chemical imbalances, as well as their loved ones, can also reap benefits from this knowledge, realizing there is hope. I believe that all who read this book – physicians, nurses, detoxi-fication specialists, psychiatrists, and therapists, as well as patients themselves and their family members, will gain an invaluable understanding to assist individuals through the jungle of chemical dependency and psychiatric disorders to reach a new dependency-free way of life. That kind of success is the most rewarding thing we can possibly achieve in this field.

Using neurochemical schematics works, and if other medical professionals could get past the idea that these cutting-edge methods are "just a theory" and realize that our method is almost 100 percent effective, they would be more successful in helping their patients. With the amount of untold millions who suffer from addiction and psychiatric problems, as well as unsuccessful detoxifications, there is clearly room for advancement in the field of neurochemistry. Evidently there is a problem with the existing tools and therefore, a need for improvement. Validation of a method like the one I am advocating, one that is somewhat based on theory and experience, is definitely in question by scientists. However, it should be noted that every good and useful method starts out as a theory. It is only when we venture into precarious territory that we can make ad-vancement and science can forge ahead.

Brain Rules

Rule #4: Treating underlying genetic neurotransmitter deficiencies and imbalances, as well as addressing psychiatric conditions, is paramount in treating drug dependency and alcoholism.

Rule #5: Cravings are caused by an imbalance in one or more neurotransmitter systems.

"Together these neurotransmitter systems act as a global communications system with impeccable order.... It is this kind of predictable communication and behavior among neurotransmitter systems that makes my methods of treatment so successful."

Chapter 3

Neurotransmitter Basics

The brain contains billions of neurons. Each neuron con-
nects with other neurons in a very special way, much like two
people with their palms nearly touching, where one can feel the
aura of the other person. Imagine that the person on the left has
a chemical under their skin that jumps out and crosses the gap
and stimulates the other person's hand. Once that happens, the
chemical is reabsorbed back into the person's palm that originally
sent it. Those neurotransmitters, or chemical messengers, are the
chemicals responsible for transmitting nerve impulses across the
synapses of the nervous system. The transmitting palm that holds the
neurochemical represents the *presynaptic neuron*. The gap between
the palms represents the *synapse*, and the palm that is stimulated
by the transfer of the neurochemicals represents what is called the
postsynaptic neuron. The brain contains billions of these synapses,
and these micro functioning parts make up the pieces of the larger
neurotransmitter groups. Though some of these neurotransmitter
groups or systems are distributed throughout the brain while others
are located in specific areas, they are *all* connected to each other in

one way or another.

There are eight basic neurotransmitter systems that you need to familiarize yourself with: serotonin, dopamine, GABA, glutamate,

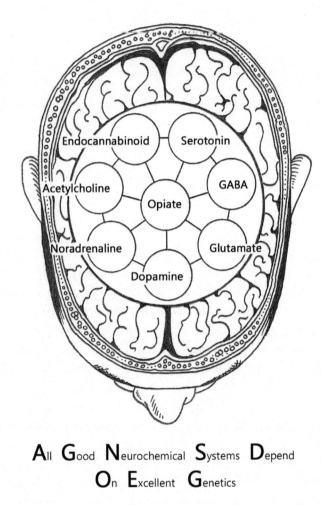

All **G**ood **N**eurochemical **S**ystems **D**epend **O**n **E**xcellent **G**enetics

There are strong connections between the eight basic neurotransmitter systems significant to chemical dependency. The placement of these eight systems in this neurotransmitter diagram will make more sense as you read on and learn how to use it. You should be able to memorize the arrangement as we go along.

opiate, noradrenergic, endocannabinoid, and acetylcholine.[3] Each of these systems consists of the neurotransmitters themselves, as well as their receptor sites and neurons. Together these neurotransmitter systems act as a global communications system with impeccable order, much like the World Wide Web, with different languages from different countries all performing executive functions. Some of the neurotransmitter systems have data language platforms and hardware that relate to each other more than others. For instance, the opiate system is closely tied to the GABA system, and later I will explain how we can manipulate one system and get a positive and remarkable response from the other. It is this kind of predictable communication and behavior among neurotransmitter systems that makes my methods of treatment so successful. I have broken down and outlined their predictability in a set of rules – rules that I base my work on.

Though we will first be examining each of these systems separately to become acquainted with how they function, bear in mind, in reality they are all very much connected to one another and adjust themselves in some reactionary balance to any changes that occur in one or the other. For now though, we will cover some basics of these eight neurotransmitter systems and afterwards, use that knowledge to expand our understanding and practice of treatment. If you are a beginner to the field neurochemistry, the content within this chapter may seem a little over-whelming at first, but I assure you, as you read on, things will start to fall into place and you will end up a neurotransmitter guru by the time you complete this book.

The Serotonin System

The serotonin system is the system that is talked about the most because of its widely recognized tie to depression; however, it is lim-

---

3 A good mnemonic device for remembering these eight different neurotransmitter systems is "All (acetylcholine) Good (GABA) Neurochemical (noradrenergic) Systems (serotonin) Depend (dopamine) On (opiate) Excellent (endocannabinoid) Genetics (glutamate)"

ited in its size and total global connections. It is centered in the edges of the mid-forebrain bundle or center of the brain, (what I like to call the *Pentium*). It is also found in blood platelets and the intestinal tract.

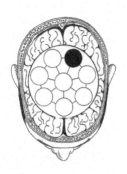

Currently there is believed to be 22, or more different serotonin types throughout the brain. There are seven main types that are each named numerically and referred to as 5-hydroxytryptamine 1 (5-HT1), 5-hydroxytryptamine 2 (5-HT2), etc. all the way through 5-hydroxytryptamine 7 (5-HT7). What make up the rest of the roughly 22 types are actually the subtypes of these main seven, which have names like 5-HT1a, 5-HT1b, and so on. These subtypes have complex functions in brain chemistry, which we unfortunately will not be addressing because it is beyond the scope of this book. Instead, the serotonin to keep your eye on is 5-HT3, since it plays an important role in addiction. The subtypes influence depression, anxiety, gut function, and effects on dopamine and other complex brain functions.

When visualizing an individual's serotonin system, it helps to imagine a piano keyboard, twenty-two keys long, with each key representing one of the serotonins: some keys are up, some down, some stuck, or some not even there. We don't know what the arrangement of each individual is without doing a brain biopsy. Some people's serotonin levels are low permanently throughout their entire life because they are born that way, yet others suffer from low levels only temporarily. This is because these neurotransmitter systems are dynamic; their levels can be affected by any number of chemicals, drugs, or hormones.

An example of a common fluctuation that occurs in serotonin is tied to premenstrual syndrome (PMS). The moodiness associated with PMS is related to the level of the hormone, estrogen and is actually the result of a temporary serotonin deficiency. Upon ovulation, there is a progressive increase in the ovaries' release of estrogen. More estrogen means higher serotonin levels. Estrogen acts near serotonin synapses as an agonistic (stimulating) modulator, modifying how much serotonin will get released into the synapse, essentially kicking out extra serotonin from the presynaptic neuron. However when the female doesn't get pregnant, the estrogen drops dramatically. Depending on the individual, this drop usually occurs anywhere from one week prior menstruation, to whenever menstruation starts. This dramatic drop in estrogen means there is no longer an extra boost of serotonin from the weakened serotonin synapse, and that is when the symptoms of PMS surface. Many recovering alcoholics suffer a relapse due to this monthly estrogen and concomitant acute serotonin drop with its resultant PMS. There has never been a study to assess whether women with more severe symptoms of PMS have family histories of alcoholism, but I believe there is a strong correlation. They are usually serotonin deficient because they are what I explain later as, *genetic alcoholics.*

Serotonin deficiency is most commonly associated with depression and anxiety as well as the frequently heard, "I can't take one more thing!" or "Don't even talk to me!!!" Most of the antidepressants, from Prozac to Celexa, raise various serotonins in different ways. I have my preferences and will discuss them later. Raising serotonin levels works well in the treatment of alcoholics, general anxiety disorders, panic attacks, depression on a general basis, PMS, and sometimes bipolar symptoms if you don't exacerbate a manic episode.

The Dopamine System

Dopamine is fun stuff. You can go on the Internet and buy dopamine. You can buy dopamine receptors. They use them for research. Lately there has been heightened interest in this system among researchers and addictionologists. There have been myriads of newly published articles on dopamine

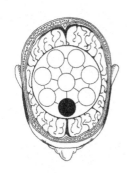

receptor sites, receptor site proliferation, and studies of how different drugs and alcohol affect this system. Knowledge of dopamine's strong ties with both the opiate and GABA system has proven quite beneficial for improving treatment for patients going through either alcohol or opiate withdrawal.

I have seen various articles telling us that dopamine is in the locus coeruleus, in the nucleus accumbens, and spreading out in the limbic system. Dopamine is the only neurotransmitter system that is not only isolated in different lower parts of the brain like the locus coeruleus, but also in the substantia nigra. Interestingly enough, feelings of depression and euphoria are both linked to dopamine levels. Scientists have done PET scans of the brain to determine if dopamine centers "light up" when experimental subjects are shown different pictures. For example, if they show you a picture of your beloved dog, everything lights up. If they show you a picture of your mother-in-law, nothing lights up. You get no dopamine response.

There are five definite types of dopamine: D1, D2, D3, D4, and D5. However, studies suggest there could be more. Methamphetamine is an agonist for stimulus to D1 and some D2 sites. Cocaine raises D2 and some D3, causing a person to become euphoric and happy. When an individual's D2 and D3 levels are too high, it can make them psychotic. Schizophrenics, in fact, are known to have problems with their D4 as well as too many D2 receptors. Recently, researchers have also discovered a link between D4 and ADHD.

As with serotonin, a person can have a genetic depletion of one or more types of their dopamine. There are medications available that will increase the amount of dopamine released in the brain. Abilify, an anti-psychotic medication, is a D2 stimulant that is almost all D2. Wellbutrin is a partial D2 agonist. Opiates cause the release of dopamine in important areas of the brain like the nucleus accumbens and the locus coeruleus. There are also a lot of dopamine blockers available that will block the various subtypes for individuals with too much dopamine who are or are on the verge of being schizophrenic or psychotic. For example, Haldol, an anti-psychotic used in alcoholic detoxifications, is a D2 inhibitor.

One must be very wary when administering treatment centered on the dopamine system, because if a patient initially has too much dopamine running through their system and they receive more, it can cause them to hallucinate or get rigid. Thus all medical staff must be familiar with which medications block and which ones increase dopamine. When treating patients with drugs that cause an increase in dopamine release, we have to be careful not to give too much of the drug. If too much is administered, side effects similar to illicit drug-induced over-stimulation of dopamine occurs, including agitation, paranoia, and bizarre behavior.

Many drug abusers seek the high associated with elevated dopamine. As mentioned above, cocaine is an agonist for D2 and D3 receptor sites. In rat studies, we have found that normal rats get a real high out of cocaine because it hits D2 receptors. Some rats do not get any effect out of cocaine because of receptor site or D2 neuron deficiencies. We also know that people who use high dose cocaine can develop cocaine-induced psychosis because of the high output of dopamine in the brain. Likewise, in methamphetamine use, a similar psychosis can result from the high output of dopamine and noradrenaline.

Dopamine is a key player when handling various problems, whether they are self-incurred or naturally occurring. Its imbalance can be part of the problem, yet it can be utilized to arrive at solutions. Depression non-responsive to treatment with serotonin agonists can often be effectively treated with concomitant D2 drugs. Bipolar disorder and schizophrenia both appear to be tied to some dopamine imbalance.

So there you have it – too much dopamine will cause one to hallucinate or become psychotic, but not enough can cause one to become depressed. There exists a fine balance between how much dopamine is necessary to feel good and how much will make a person delusional. The dopamine agonist drugs used to regulate dopamine release therefore must be carefully adjusted so as not to get unwanted side effects. The two most important things for you to understand about dopamine are (1) dopamine is one of the three central neurotransmitters systems closely tied to depression and (2) dopamine is an absolutely vital and extensively effective neurotransmitter in chemical dependency treatment.

The GABA System

The GABA system is the calming force within the brain. Though recent studies of rats reveal that GABA is heavily concentrated in the globus pallidus, GABA is actually found throughout the brain. It acts to "put the brakes" on any fast moving neuronal activity. When GABA is activated, it is as if one hundred million stop signs in the brain pop up. Some people inherit a lot of GABA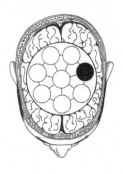
and some do not. I personally did not get much GABA. I talk fast, move fast, and am currently writing this sentence at lightning speed. People that have general anxiety disorder (GAD) probably don't have much GABA either, or they may have a lot of glutamate or noradrenaline; GABA balances out those more agitating neurotransmitters. Of all the neurotransmitter systems, this is the one I use the most in treatments. It is very predictable and quite rewarding to use. If medical professionals activate the right receptor sites and know which sites to leave alone, they have successful treatments.

Science reveals there are at least five types of GABA receptor sites, however other than the GABA1a site (the "first site"), no one has consistently named the other sites.[4] Certain GABA agonist drugs specifically work on one type of GABA receptor site, and other drugs work on the other individual sites. The sites could be randomly placed throughout the brain and when they are activated by the medications we give, they serve as an inhibitor of rapid nerve

---

4 The *GABA1a* site is also referred to as the *GABA a1* site.

conduction, thereby opposing glutamate. To clarify, let's address the GABA1a site, the first site of the system.

Administering diazepam (that is Valium, an anti-anxiety medication in the benzodiazepine family) activates GABA1a sites, causing the whole brain to calm down. Since 1957 when Roche labs first made Valium, there are now nearly 300 renditions or pharmaceutical products made from the original molecule. It appears they all activate that GABA1a site. That GABA1a site is unfortunately, a nightmare for addictionologists everywhere.

At first, the brain's reaction to the stimulation of this GABA1a site is very predictable, but after a few years, it becomes highly *unpredictable*, even causing a paradoxical effect and actually inciting agitation. As the dosage increases and the GABA1a sites get inundated with more and more Valium product, the system gains tolerance and the receptor sites eventually become disabled, leaving the agitating glutamate system unopposed. Essentially these Valium products, when over-used, render the GABA neurotransmitter system ineffective or cancelled out. I see this scenario quite frequently when patients are in the ICU getting massive doses of the benzodiazepine Ativan or Versed. The more drugs administered, the more the system becomes defunct, leaving patients with global agitation. The patients most at risk for this reaction are those who have taken Valium or benzodiazepines in the past and then receive doctor-ordered benzodiazepines after a surgery.

Beware! You must remember that the GABA1a site is very unpredictable. Ninety-nine percent of the time, I am discontinuing drugs that hit the GABA1a site and using other receptor sites in the GABA system to calm or detoxify the patient. The other four GABA sites are much more predictable. Let us call these sites GABA 2, GABA 3, GABA 4, and GABA 5. Barbiturates or phenobarbital is a GABA drug, and I picture it hitting the GABA 2 site. We use it to detoxify patients off benzodiazepines. I call GABA 3 the GABA-like site for certain drugs that act like GABA to that specific site. Robaxin and baclofen also seem to be GABA-like, and they may stimulate the GABA 4 site. All the other anti-seizure drugs like De-pakote, Topamax, Lamictal, and Tegretol activate the GABA 5 site.

As you can see, we have a lot of options to get the inhibitory effects of GABA, all without hitting the GABA 1a site. Using the above-mentioned drugs causes this inhibitory effect everywhere when activating the GABA receptors. The GABA1a site seems to be the most powerful site of them all, but the strength of the other four sites, when activated in unison, has the same total brain inhibitory affect, equal to that of the GABA1a site. To overcome the agitation that results from stopping the benzodiazepines from hitting the GABA1a site, these other four sites must be hit. However, use caution with phenobarbital because of the dangers of tolerance. Many doctors abuse this drug. We will examine the repercussions of this later.

What happens to the GABA system during detoxification is often a strong determinant of the detoxification's outcome. Picture this: You have a receptor site that all the benzodiazepine drugs hit and activate when molecules of the drug are bouncing in and out of that receptor site. You can block that site by adding a drug that has an affinity for that same site and it will actually crowd out the action of the benzodiazepine. Romazicon, flumazenil is an example of a GABA1a site competitive inhibitor that deactivates GABA. It does so by hugging the site, without activating it. So if someone has overdosed on Valium and you want to wake him or her up, you can add flumazenil to block the site from the Valium, and the patient wakes up. The reaction you get in the brain is equivalent to covering up all the stop signs in the world at once, leaving all the crazy fast drivers running around uninhibited. Unfortunately, if the person is benzodiazepine dependent, that inactivation could cause that individual to have seizures.

In the past, some addictionologists up-regulated the GABA system by doing exactly that – injecting the competitive inhibitor flumazenil into the brain via the venous system, thereby blocking billions of GABA sites suddenly. That can cause sudden benzodiazepine withdrawal and marked unopposed agitation of the brain and seizure activity. The reasoning behind wanting to suddenly up-regulate the GABA site is somewhat similar to the rapid detoxification of the opiate system with Narcan or naltrexone. I have not used flumazenil myself, since the GABA1a site is so erratic and volatile. Such a high amount of uncertainty carries increased risk. The risk lies within the unopposed glutamate, bringing us to our next neurotransmitter system.

The Glutamate System

Glutamate is one of the most ubiquitous neurotransmitters in the brain. It is located throughout the entire cortex. If there is an agitating aspect of the brain, this is the culprit. I often liken glutamate to NASCAR stockcars circling 'round and 'round in the brain, revving it up. What balances that out is a lot of stop signs from the GABA system, which is almost as ubiquitous. If an individual has low glutamate, he or she will not have much agitation, especially if his or her

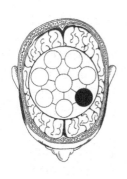

GABA levels are normal or high. It is as if GABA and glutamate are on a teeter-totter in a balancing act of the brain. Fully grasping the significance of this delicate balance that exists between the glutamate and GABA systems is absolutely vital to understanding both alcoholism and how to facilitate safe and successful alcohol detoxifications.

Alcohol, among other things, increases levels of glutamate over time. Eventually the brain can become so agitated by this elevated glutamate that a grand mal seizure will occur, especially if the glutamate levels are not opposed by a sufficient amount of GABA. Alcoholics in acute withdrawal have high glutamate levels and lower GABA levels. They also have low magnesium and potassium serum levels. Traditionally when intramuscular or intravenous magne-

sium is admin-
istered, the pa-
tient seems to
be less agitated,
as though glu-
tamate is being
suppressed. If
you are a physi-
cian adminis-
tering magne-
sium to an agi-
tated alcoholic
in withdrawal,
take note of that
phenomenon.
It is extremely
important for
alcoholic indi-
viduals trying
to quit drinking
to take a mag-
nesium supple-
ment because
m a g n e s i u m
helps to elimi-

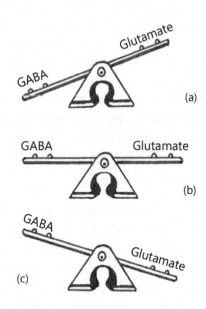

These diagrams demonstrate the balances between GABA and glutamate that exist in...

(a) a highly agitated person
(b) a person with an average temperament, neither overly agitated, nor exceedingly calm
(c) a very calm person

nate the overstimulation of the brain and heart.

Imagine a teeter-totter with a fulcrum in the middle, GABA on one side and glutamate on the other. In people with normal levels, these two opposing neurotransmitters are balanced, with their teeter-totter being level (as shown in Image b). Over time when one consumes alcohol with increased tolerance and use, the alcohol gradually causes an imbalance of GABA and glutamate by steadily increasing the brain's overall glutamate levels. The GABA, on the other hand, bounces up and down daily as an individual drinks. Typically alcohol raises GABA immediately to decrease the agitation from the ever-increasing glutamate levels. That process, in chemical dependency neurophysiology circles, is called *kindling*. It is no wonder that the alcoholic has to drink non-stop to keep the shakes under control; the alcoholic drinks daily or all the time in order to keep the GABA up at a level to counteract the glutamate. When they don't drink, the GABA drops, leaving behind dangerously high glutamate levels with the person's brain going into hyperdrive, possibly causing shakes, racing thoughts, sweating, or even convulsing and seizing (which is called an *alcohol withdrawal seizure*).

So in a sense, alcoholics that continuously drink are self-medicating themselves to avoid going into withdrawal and to prevent seizures. They are essentially using the alcohol to keep their GABA elevated. In order to get them off the alcohol, we employ other methods that raise the GABA high enough to slow things down and pre-

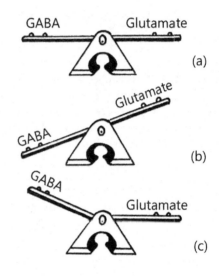

These three diagrams represent the GABA-glutamate balance for a non-genetic alcoholic...

(a) before he picks up the habit of drinking
(b) once he is an active alcoholic, with no drink in his system and craving alcohol
(c) after he has a few drinks in his systems

Thus alcoholics continue to drink in order to combat the agitation that accompanies elevated glutamate.

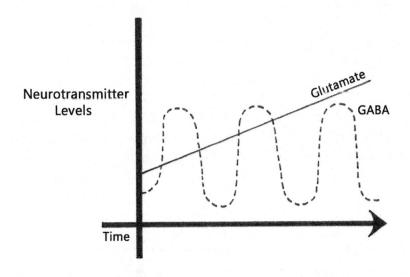

While the GABA levels bounce up and down with each drink, the glutamate levels of an alcoholic steadily increase over time, remaining elevated even when the individual is not under the influence of alcohol. The alcoholic finds him or herself drinking more and more in order to raise the GABA enough to keep up with the ever-increasing glutamate.

vent seizures. We do this by using the five GABA sites medicinally to oppose the glutamate, thereby controlling the detoxification process. This makes them feel comfortable and more importantly, prevents alcohol withdrawal seizures. Most of the time when using these methods, glutamate starts to drop on its own by the third day, seeking its innate balance. It will continue to drop over the next two months.

The best way to control high levels of glutamate is to increase GABA levels by stimulating GABA sites (not including the GABA1a site) as much as possible. Campral is a new drug that seems to decrease glutamate over time and decrease cravings. Another development to keep an eye on is any research involving the NMDA system. NMDA is a glutamate receptor complex, an activator with a glutamate receptor on it, along with five or more receptors for magnesium, zinc, PCP and dextromethorphan. The reason I bring this up is that glutamate is very toxic to the brain and can cause brain damage, especially if unopposed by GABA. However, the magnesium receptor site on the NMDA seems to calm glutamate agitation. To date, NMDA research is incomplete, and therefore impractical in my clinical work. In the future, after further research into how I can orchestrate its receptor sites to my advantage, I can see its potential. Regardless, what is clear about the glutamate system now is that it is closely tied to the GABA system and the GABA system, in turn, is closely tied to the opiate system. Confused? Just keep reading and you will get it. Now let's talk about the opiate system.

The Opiate System

Our own natural opiate system is made up of receptor sites throughout the brain, the spinal cord, and the periphery of the body. Having these opiate receptor sites means that your body also produces its own opiate chemical that activates those sites. There are several types of opiates, but let's keep it simple and call these naturally produced opiate chemicals, *endorphins* (short for endogenous morphine). Morphine, codeine, and synthetic opiates also activate these receptor sites. Heroin (diacetylmorphine) is an example of a drug that is metabolized into morphine and codeine, and is abused by individuals for the euphoric effect of rapidly increased opiate release.

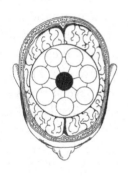

Opiate abuse in its many different forms is rampant throughout our society for various reasons (the most common of which will be discussed in chapter 11). My experience with the opiate system is definitely different from that of other pain management specialists and practitioners. After 10,000 opiate detoxifications, I have gained insight, as well as a lot of respect for how neurotransmitter systems are integrated. For instance, when opiates activate the opiate system, they then activate the GABA system, which in turn stimulates the dopamine system. I have utilized this kind of knowledge to develop what I refer to as the *back door method* to opiate detoxification. Many are solely aware of the most obvious approach, the front door method, where doctors stimulate the opiate system by administering narcotics that hit the opiate sites directly.[5] At present, it is widely accepted that the only way to detoxify someone off narcotics is through the front door, where other narcotics that are agonists and antagonists for opiates are prescribed and then gradually tapered off. In fact, as addiction medicine specialists, we have been trained to only look at one neurotransmitter system at a time and not the unsuspected latent relationships that exist among them. This, however, is a huge oversight because these relationships are much more profound than we have ever assumed.

When using this back door method to detoxify patients off opiates, there is no need to administer any direct opiate stimulants or narcotics. I know this because I use this back door method every day, several times a day. Instead of using the front door method, which involves directly stimulating the opiate system with medicinal drugs like Suboxone, Subutex, and Methadone, the back door method directly stimulates the opiate system's partner– the GABA system. Utilizing this back door method is especially necessary in order to prevent patients from trading in their old opiate addictions for new addictions to their opiate medications. We are essentially playing the game of neurotransmitter relationships and exploiting the strong underlying connection between the GABA and opiate systems.

The GABA system is an exceedingly powerful and dominant system with a very impressive connection to the opiate system; in fact, the opiate and GABA systems are like a loving man and

---

5 *Narcotics* is a term used in reference to opiates. Narcotics hit the opiate aspect of the brain where there are Mu receptors. Heroin, morphine, Oxy-Contin, Dilaudid, Demerol, Darvocet, fentanyl Talwin, and codeine are all examples of narcotics.

wife holding hands. The man in this illustration, the opiate system, is in detoxification and unable to speak and is holding hands with the wife, the GABA system. In the back door method, we talk to her and stimulate her while he listens intensely. Being connected with that inherent association calms him down.

By stimulating all receptor sites of the GABA system, we have successfully discontinued the use

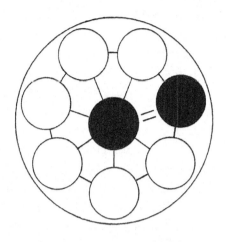

When using the back door method to detoxify people off of opiates, I make use of the strong relationship that exists between the opiate and GABA systems. By using medications that stimulate GABA production, the opiate system in turn gets stimulated in a non-addictive manner.

of narcotics and detoxified thousands of Methadone, OxyContin, and heroin addicts. In a mere five days we can bring the opiate system in for a soft landing, like a troubled aircraft safely hitting the runway. Without using narcotics when detoxifying heavy narcotic-use patients, we have successfully helped thousands of patients with various pain issues (such as chronic back pain, migraines, and so on) to conquer their addiction to drugs and pain-killers. In cases of opiate withdrawal, stimulating the GABA system has a two-fold purpose. Not only does it back-feed into the opiate system, it also effectively opposes the glutamate. Where the front door method of using drugs such as Suboxone or Subutex won't work, stimulating GABA in the back door method of opiate detoxification works *every* time.[6]

The opiate system is also stimulated by alcohol. Drinking alcohol at moderate levels causes pleasure and contentment. As one drinks more and more, the blood alcohol level rises, and eventually an opiate sense of well-being is reached that is extremely euphoric and equally addictive. Physiologically, the nucleus accumbens area of the brain is being activated and endorphins and dopamine are released. The extremely pleasurable feeling accompanying this dopamine and opiate release drives the alcoholic to keep drinking in order to titrate the alcohol within this narrow margin. Trying to remain at this level of euphoric intoxication is difficult though since there is a small margin between reinforcing this feeling of euphoria and drinking to the point of blacking out. Some alcoholics readily drink until they find that level of intoxication because the endogenous opiates and dopamine are so addictive. In doing so, more often than not the drinker overdoses and blacks out.

These alcoholics who drink to chase the opiate and dopamine surge and ultimately overdose, leading to loss of cognizance, are known as *blackout drinkers*. Many genetic alcoholics fit into this category. They sometimes end up using narcotics, giving them the same effect, and then they no longer need to drink alcohol. We refer to these patients as being *cross-addicted*. Actually, *across-the-brain-to-another-imbalanced-neurotransmitter-system* would be a more explicit term. Opiate blockers are advantageous when treating these blackout drinkers. Narcan and naltrexone are competitive inhibitors that block the opiate receptors and dopamine release. Studies have shown that the use of these drugs increase the sobriety rate up to three times compared to those given a placebo alone.

---

6 Suboxone and Subutex are drugs commonly used by doctors to detoxify patients off of opiates with some success; however, these drugs have addictive properties of their own.

The Noradrenergic System

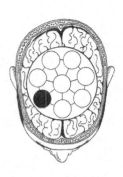

The noradrenergic neurotransmitter system is integral for learning and also for negative thoughts and emotions such as fear and anxiety. It is associated with norepinephrine and its stimulating effects, but as a neurotransmitter, is called *noradrenaline*. The noradrenergic system is limited in its presence within the brain. It is found in the lower part of the brain called the *locus coeruleus* and is also very prominent in the fear center of the brain called the *amygdala*. Incessant nightmares, like the kind of night terrors that a soldier might get of grotesque battle scenes, come out of this fear center excited by noradrenaline. Quite frequently I see doctors prescribe high dose noradrenergic drugs to people with night terrors, and I wonder if that is in fact making the amygdala even worse. Fortunately we are able to use alpha adrenergic blockers to calm the amygdala and change people's lives for the better.

Noradrenaline is vital for reduction of pain, especially the pain of fibromyalgia, back pain, and pain in the legs from diabetes or other causes where nerves fire inappropriately. When noradrenaline drugs such as Cymbalta, Effexor, Savella, or Pristiq are given, weird things happen in the spinal fluid where the brain bathes and the nerves exist. Within the spinal fluid, noradrenaline starts rising and the pain coming from the nerves decreases. It is fascinating to see this neuronal effect coming from this measurable change in the neurotransmitter, noradrenaline.

Noradrenaline is closely tied to the GABA system. When benzodiazepines (any minor tranquilizers that among other things counter anxiety and convulsions) are administered, activating the GABA system, an anxiolytic effect is created, and the release of noradrenaline is inhibited in the locus coeruleus. Tricyclic antidepressants also inhibit the release of noradrenaline. Trazodone, one of those tricyclic antidepressants, is a useful medicine for sleep because it inhibits the noradrenergic effect and therefore acts as a sedative. For this reason, we use trazodone in the withdrawal state of alcohol and opiate detoxifications. Seroquel is a close second in that category of antidepressants. I have found it beneficial to use noradrenergic drugs sparingly in the acute detoxification phase. We know that Wellbutrin has a seizure risk factor of roughly 0.4 percent when one receives over 450mg/day. That is one reason why we always stop Wellbutrin during acute alcohol withdrawal. Then we add GABA drugs to decrease seizure risk. Tegretol seems to be a good GABA drug. It has proven to be an integral part of our detoxification arsenal. At 200mg twice a day, Tegretol has successfully prevented all seizures in twenty thousand detoxifications.

The noradrenergic system is a difficult neurochemical system to get a handle on. When glutamate hyper-agitation is occurring, it is difficult to differentiate what is glutamate and what is noradrenaline. Sure you could say that the fear is more adrenergic, but it is hard to buy that concept when you see a patient really in withdrawal from alcohol or having a panic attack. I add noradrenaline to the therapeutic regimen of extremely lethargic and depressed patients, the kind of patients who hardly ever get off the couch and wouldn't be afraid until the place was on fire. Cymbalta, Effexor, Pristiq, and Wellbutrin all have some noradrenergic effects. Although some doctors will give noradrenaline to patients with anxiety, I am wary of this method. They have had the experience that in a state of anxiety, Cymbalta will calm the patient down. I am not sure how that works; perhaps it decreases agitated depression, or has different effects in different people due to their unique neurochemical balances.

Wellbutrin is an antidepressant. Its generic name is *bupropion*. It is one of the few drugs that will raise three neurotransmitters: noradrenaline, acetylcholine, and dopamine. Of these three effected neurotransmitters, noradrenaline is the most agitating. The dopamine in bupropion is an important antidepressant. The noradrenaline also works as an antidepressant. Although it is only my opinion, my experience has led me to conclude that serotonin and dopamine are the systems most useful in battling depression, followed closely by the noradrenaline system.

The Endocannabinoid System

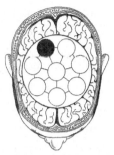

Yes, we do indeed have receptor sites throughout the brain that cannabis activates. But remember, if you have the receptor site in your brain, then you also *naturally* produce the chemical that is going to activate that receptor. If we have insulin receptors, then we have insulin. If we have estrogen receptors, then we produce estrogen. There are probably 400 types of receptors on cells or nerves and you can expect to find 400 substances that our body produces to activate those receptors. It just so happens that there are substances, chemicals, or drugs that are produced outside our body (exogenous) that will *also* activate or inhibit those same sites to one degree or another. It takes a greater quantity of an exogenous substance to activate the system than that of a natural endogenous agonist. It only seems logical that a naturally produced substance in the body would be a perfect key to unlock and activate a receptor site. Such is the case with cannabis. Our own cannabis activates the system the best.

There are two different endocannabinoids, labeled CB1 and CB2, with "CB" standing for "cannabinoid." The CB2 receptor sites are usually found in the periphery of the body and are involved in pain control issues. CB1 is tied to the sensation of appetite. It is found all through the brain and when activated, gives us what some recognize as the "marijuana munchies." One theory is that when the body is in need of fuel, the gut starts producing CB1 agonists that are then circulated in the blood, making you feel hungry. When the bowel is full, it shuts off and the munchies are gone. CB1 is also tied to some forms of depression. If there is inadequate CB1 activation, a person can get very depressed and even suicidal.

There is a theory that gastric bypass surgery done in a Roux-n-Y method can lead to deficiencies of the CB1 activation due to the blind loop not having any food access and no CB1 output. The endocannabinoid system, interestingly enough, is also activated with alcohol, and it is not uncommon for the gastric outlet patients with a strong family history of alcoholism, to suddenly become active alcoholics. One theorized reason behind this occurrence is that these patients now have to depend on alcohol to strike CB1 receptors in the brain directly to satisfy the cravings that were previously satisfied by food in the gut. Within three months after a gastric bypass patient has had their stomach surgically downsized and the intestine switched around, alcohol goes through much more quickly than any food can and is rapidly absorbed. This leads to accelerated alcohol blood levels, intoxication, and a huge, highly euphoric dopamine release. This has been experienced by many gastric bypass patients who are genetically endowed with neurotransmitter imbalances.

Some gastric surgeons are starting to take notice of this correlation. Many are still puzzled at the event of this complication after their surgery. A few doctors have started screening for a predisposition towards alcoholism by examining family genetics, but others unjustifiably believe that these kinds of patients simply had a food addiction that turned into an alcohol addiction. There are several interesting theories to this disruptive and serious chemical dependency problem. It is very complex, so I am still searching for a clear answer.

As an addictionologist, it is good to know the endocannabinoid system; however, knowing that it is activated by alcohol and being familiar with its effect on gastric bypass patients is a challenge. I do not currently have much use for this neurochemical system in detoxification or in treatment of psychiatric states and will continue not to until more research and other agonistic agents or blockers become available.

The Acetylcholine System

Acetylcholine is found in the brain and peripheral nerves. As new research reveals how acetylcholine is integrated into the other

systems, it may prove to be increasingly helpful in detoxifications. At present, we know
that acetylcholine is vital for memory and
plays a key role in the treatment of demen-
tia. New evidence from Suzuki K. indicates
that acetylcholine activity is deficient in the
fusiform gyrus of individuals with autism
spectrum disorders (ASD). Interestingly
enough, nicotine activates acetylcholine,
along with dopamine and noradrenaline.

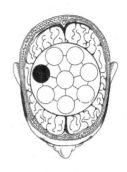

Wellbutrin will also activate the same neurotransmitters in a somewhat similar fashion. This system is good to know because of its
benefits in treating nicotine dependency and a few unusual types
of depression. Those situations are the only occasions in which I
currently use the acetylcholine system.

The Neurotransmitter Systems'
Interdependence and Influence

These eight neurotransmitter systems are the inherited systems
that both illicit drugs and prescription medications influence with
either an agonistic (stimulate) or an antagonistic (inhibitory) effect. Once you learn the ins and outs of these systems and talk
with a patient, you will start to recognize which systems are having
a notable influence on the person. If there is an over-abundance
or deficiency in any of the systems, it will become apparent. You
might even start to notice that a friend or family member has higher
or lower levels of one neurochemical or another, explaining some
personality characteristic you have always just accepted as normal
for that individual. Many times when talking with a patient, I will
write out the eight systems and make notes next to them, giving
explanations as to how they apply to this patient and why certain
medications would be effective.

It is vital to remember that all of the neurotransmitter systems
are made up of billions of neurons that are not separated into inde-

pendent areas like continents or countries. Rather, in some ways they are more like a mixed salad. It is as if they are different nations that are somewhat independent, but also connected in very consistent ways to make an overall executive system. Some countries are more dependent on one another than others. The result of the recent stock market crash on Wall Street is a perfect demonstration of the kind of interdependence that also exists among our neurotransmitter systems. When the crash occurred, many other worldwide stock exchanges also crashed within days. China and Russia had to shut down their exchanges to stop the panic. That event made it evident that any damage to the USA would spark repercussions around the globe. That is essentially what happens to the brain's neurochemical systems. These eight neurotransmitter systems are in constant communication with one another; hitting one system in the brain causes repercussions and changes throughout all the other systems. This is a very important concept to bear in mind.

Many individuals do not realize just how far-reaching the effects of drugs and medications are. The effects of cocaine and methamphetamine, for example, are not just limited to the dopamine system. The same rule applies to medications. Most physicians and pharmaceutical companies only stress the importance of a medication's effect on perhaps the serotonin system or opiate system and proceed as if its effect is restricted to just those one or two particular systems. That is a dire oversimplification and quite frankly, not true. Physicians have recently injected flumazenil, a blocker of GABA, into the brain in attempt to up-regulate the GABA system. These MD's have found that this sudden blockade of GABA affected the other systems with some strange results, for instance, changing people's cravings. In a complex system such as the brain, while there is consistency, you never really know exactly what effect you are going to get because every brain is wired a little different from the next. The main concept to keep in mind is that the brain has global executive functioning, and every medicine and street drug has a variable effect that will likely reverberate throughout the other neurotransmitter systems.

Brain Rules

Rule #6: The brain has eight important genetically hardwired basic neurotransmitter systems that medical professionals should become familiar with: serotonin, dopamine, GABA, glutamate, opiate, noradrenaline, endocannabinoid, and acetylcholine.

Rule #7: These neurotransmitter systems are interconnected; if one system becomes altered, the others are affected as well. Some systems' relationships are stronger than others.

Rule #8: A paradoxical effect occurs after too many benzodiazepines have been prescribed to a patient, actually inciting agitation, because tolerance has been built up at the GABA1a site and there is no longer enough GABA stimulation to counteract the patient's glutamate.

"Realizing that the inclination towards drug abuse and alcoholism is inherited is the first step towards administering the highest standard of treatment."

Chapter 4

Genetics:
The Source of Addiction

People ask me, "When is an alcoholic an alcoholic?" The answer: the moment the zygote is formed. Each one of us is born with genetically ordained levels of the chemicals that run throughout our nervous system – neurotransmitters. Some of us are born with an imbalance of those chemicals. In search of a correction for that imbalance, these individuals often turn to drugs or alcohol – anything that will make them feel "normal." Thus the imbalance causes cravings, and cravings lead to actions that result in chemical dependency. The drugs that they crave are those that affect the deficient or imbalanced neurotransmitter systems that they inherited from their parents.

Recently the scientists and researchers at the National Institute of Drug Abuse (NIDA) stated that at least 50 percent of the cause of addiction is due to genetic inheritance. Other studies led scientists to conclude that the influence of genetics was approximately 50 to 80 percent. Whatever the percentage, we know that genetics provide the directions for establishing each individual's neurochemical systems. In order to treat or prevent chemical dependency, we must not ignore the underlying genetic problem, but rather address it head on for the utmost effective and successful treatment. This means successful detoxifications with minimal relapses.

Inheritance of Chemical Dependency Problems

Everyone wants to blame someone else for anything they do wrong, and that is especially true when it comes to using drugs and alcohol. Well guess what? You *can* blame someone. As a matter of fact, you can blame two people – your parents.

One only needs to look at the example of schizophrenia to understand the role that *both* genetics and environment can play in a hereditary disease of the brain. Studies of individuals with certain mental illnesses, such as schizophrenia, have shown that approximately 80 percent of their present problem is neurochemical, a result of what I like to call their inherited *genetic hardware*. The environmental impact that pushes them over the edge is only the remaining 20 percent of the problem. Likewise, all that is needed to become an active alcoholic is environmental exposure to alcohol, and that is where it all starts.

After interviewing 20,000 patients and asking them about their parents, grandparents, and siblings, I have found strong correlations indicating that things such as opiate abuse, alcohol abuse, and bipolar disease often run in the family. When I talk to a patient about their parents and other family members, I try to find out if any of them are or were alcoholics or opiate abusers. I also make an effort to find out if anyone in the family is bipolar or suffering from some mental or behavioral disorder found in the DSM-IV such as Attention Deficit Hyperactivity Disorder (ADHD) or Obsessive-Compulsive Disorder (OCD). Ninety to ninety-five percent of the time, I have found that the alcoholics and addicts admitted to my unit have families with alcoholics, addicts, or some mental disorder. Hence, drug addiction is more than just environmental, more than just a string of life choices: rather, it is *genetic*.

In my investigations, rarely will I come up with nothing. They may say everyone is normal, and I think to myself, "Impossible! How could a blackout drinker with three driving under the influence (DUI) charges have no positive family history?" Usually if I dig deep enough, I find out that maybe the person was adopted and did not initially disclose that information, or perhaps his or her family was Mormon and they had the genes, but they just never drank. Sometimes I will find that everyone but the parents was riddled with alcoholism or bipolar disease. The positive trend is most likely there; you just have to dig for it.

Basic Genetics

We have 46 chromosomes within the nucleus of every one of our cells. To make things simple, we get 23 chromosomes from each parent. Those chromosomes contain DNA, the directions for forming a human being. When the sperm fertilizes the egg, the genetic information from both parents combines to form a zygote. That fertilized egg, or zygote, divides thirty times to form a baby.

For years, scientists turned to genetics to try to find the cause of alcoholism. They recognized that there was a strong genetic predisposition to inheriting alcoholism, so they made it their goal to find the gene responsible, calling it the D2 gene.[7] But their pursuit proved unsuccessful and they never found it. They started a lot of research in the 1990's when President Clinton was excited about the advent of the computer industry. He made the bold statement that this decade would be the decade of the brain, thereby paving the way for great advancements.

The recent book, *Genome: The Autobiography of a Species in 23 Chapters*, by Matt Ridley helped us to understand some of the complexity of DNA. It looked into human chromosomes and how they determine the formation of our bodies and the structure of

---

7 This name has nothing to do with D2 Dopamine.

our brains. His research made it evident that a person may not inherit the genes that encode for an adequate amount of neurons and neurotransmitters, thus predisposing a person to alcoholism. Accordingly, somewhere in the nucleotides of inherited DNA, there exists the code to construct the parts of the brain responsible for the predisposition to addiction. This area of the brain is called the *limbic system* or more specifically, the *mid forebrain bundle.*

Neuroanatomy Basics

Studying the brain's anatomy can get pretty complex. For simplicity's sake, I often liken the brain to a computer, and at the center of the brain is the mid forebrain bundle, which I like to call the *human Pentium* or *CPU*. The DNA we inherit from our parents determines the formation and contents of this so-called Pentium. This little inherited device integrates and processes information like a central processing unit (CPU). But instead of being like a computer CPU that is fixed, the human processing unit is dynamic in its ability to vary its data processing, depending on the drugs or alcohol affecting it.[8] There is a "steering wheel," so to speak, that is connected to the CPU. That steering wheel is better known as the *pleasure pathway* of the nuclei, which forms areas that are full of neurotransmitters like the locus coeruleus and ventral tegmental areas. Those areas are connected to other parts of the nucleus accumbens full of dopamine and integrated into the opiate neurochemical system. We inherit the directions to how each of those areas is to be formed; they are essentially our brain's hardware.

We inherit neuron complexes full of dopamine, serotonin, GABA, opiate, noradrenaline, endocannabinoid, acetylcholine, and glutamate; likewise, we can also inherit *deficiencies* in these neuron complexes or their connections. You may wish to read Stephen M. Stahl's book, *Essential Psychopharmacology: Neuroscientific Basis and*

---

8 This subject will be covered in greater detail in chapter 9, "Memory and Chemical Dependency".

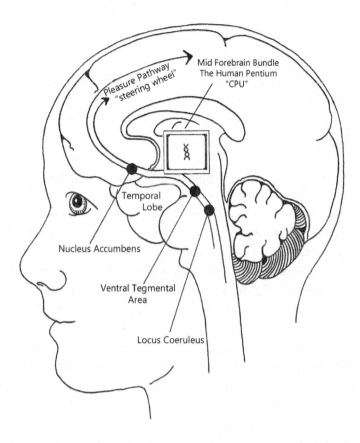

We inherit the instructions to how each part of the brain, including neuron complexes filled with neurotransmitters, is formed. We can also inherit deficiencies in those neurotransmitter levels.

Practical Applications, for more explicit information on these connections. We however will not concentrate on the synapse of nerve cells and their neurochemical functions. While it is important to know these basics of communication among individual nerve cells because they are essential for the study of micro neurophysiology, in this book, we are focusing more on the *global* function of the brain. We will look at the macro interactions of neurotransmitter systems and how they relate to behavior and various states of diseases. We will also examine which medications are most effective, using a set of principles that you will learn throughout this book.

Even though neuroanatomy is complex and often difficult to grasp, the way I am explaining it makes it more comprehensible, and therefore easier for patients and their doctors to work together to solve problems. I use this new understanding clinically in my practice every day. Both patients and those involved in their treatment need to know that being alcoholic or drug dependent does not necessarily mean that they are psychologically impaired. Rather, because of genetics, they are likely neurochemically impaired, or as I like to explain it, they are "wired wrong." This means that within that patient's Pentium/CPU, the red wire is going to the red wire, but the green wire is going to the purple wire.

Studies regarding mental illness point us to the realization that drug abuse and psychiatric disorders are the result of different genetic predispositions, which seems to have a lot of variables. Not everyone has just one single diagnosis or condition. An individual can have several neurochemical abnormalities. It is as if there are layers of them, with some more dominant than others. Resolving drug dependency problems can sometimes unearth an underlying mental disorder. Between layers of psychiatric disorders, chemical dependency, and drug abuse, it can be quite a challenge to discern exactly what genetic hardware and neurochemical state exists within the brain of an individual. No two human brains are the same, and personally I do not know if I have ever met a "normal" person… Except my wife, that is.

So there you have it – genetic alcoholics and substance abusers are wired wrong, and figuring out their genetic configuration is paramount to understanding how their brains work, and how to fix them. The good news is that there is hope for the neurochemically impaired. There are medications out there that can, with proper analysis, work with accuracy to ameliorate these disorders.

The Art of Brain Chemical Treatment

Realizing that the inclination towards drug abuse and alcoholism is inherited is the first step towards administering the highest standard of treatment. That realization motivates us to seek out the familial history of our patients, so we can better understand how each patient is wired. It is of the utmost importance for clinicians of chemical dependency and psychiatry to find out what kind of hardware exists within the brain of each patient. Due to genetics, the patient's brain is likely neurochemically out of balance, and the drugs or alcohol that they are abusing is their attempt at making up for that genetic discrepancy.

Doctors need to start thinking in terms of neurochemical balances before prescribing a treatment plan. Currently many clinicians begin their treatment by talking with their patient and analyzing the content, and then they come up with a reasonable diagnosis of one of the many typical Disorders listed in the DSM -IV. They then prescribe the drug that is indicated to treat the disorder. Instead of stopping there, it is imperative for modern clinicians to consider two more pieces to the puzzle. They need to find out the patient's family history and figure out what the individual is chemically lacking and why. They must ask themselves: What deficiencies is this patient trying to make up for with the drugs or alcohol he is using? Which neurotransmitters is she low in or all-together lacking? How can I replace those addictive substances with non-addictive medications so that the patient is more stable and does not feel the need to "treat himself"? That, my friends, is the art of brain chemical treatment.

If you do not treat the underlying genetic chemical imbalance and/or psychiatric condition, you will never be able to treat the chemical dependency problem. The patient has a neurochemical imbalance or deficiency that causes whatever addiction or DSM psychiatric problem that has been diagnosed. If the proper medications are not prescribed to mitigate the deficiencies, patients will find the street drug that comes closest to "helping" them.

Searching for the Clues that Lead to Answers

Looking at a person's drug history and psychiatric state can be quite telling as to what neurotransmitter(s) he or she is deficient in. Just the other day, I admitted a patient who was suffering from an obvious mood disorder, as well as alcoholism. This information indicated she was likely a genetic alcoholic with a serotonin deficiency. Her psychiatric state led me to consider bipolar disease. People suffering from bipolar disorder have dopaminergic problems. When she told me cocaine was the only drug that ever made her feel *normal*, that clenched it. Taking all these clues into consideration, I was able to determine where there were deficiency problems. The above-mentioned statement was very telling and vital to my diagnosis because cocaine is a powerful dopamine stimulant. Although she was no longer using cocaine, she is evidently genetically deficient in one or more dopaminergic receptor types or system balances. This meant I needed to address her dopamine deficiency along with her treatment of alcoholism and bipolar disease.

The type and severity of response each person has to drugs is determined by their genetics. Take for example cocaine. Cocaine is a drug that goes directly into the brain and activates D2 (and some D3) receptor sites, thereby increasing dopamine nerve activation. Studies have shown that just as with humans, there are rats that are born lacking normal levels of dopamine. Dopamine is one of the neurotransmitter groups that doctors can alter. There are also rats that, due to their genetics, do not respond to cocaine. When the scientists give them cocaine, they walk around the cage like "normie" rats (normal rats without any neurochemical imbalance). Scientists were baffled at this when other rats given cocaine were "loaded," experiencing all the normal side effects of cocaine. The person, or rat in this case, who has virtually no reaction to cocaine is not going to become a cocaine addict. This study confirms the importance of looking at a patient's family history since individuals' reactions to drugs vary according to their genetic predisposition.

The inclination towards opiate addiction can also be inherited.

Recent evidence reveals that on the upper arm of the thirteenth chromosome, 2,000 genes down from the end, a particular gene sequence specific to many opiate addicts exists. The NIDA feels that this particular gene makeup is significant enough to verify that there is a genetic predisposition to the addiction of opiates. This area of DNA possibly contains the instructions for the formation of the nucleus accumbens or the area anterior to it, perhaps causing an imbalance of either receptor sites or endogenous morphine (endorphins), or a combination of the two. Nevertheless, I see even more genetic family trends in alcoholism than in opiate abuse.

Alcohol raises at least five neurochemical types and a sixth when taken in high doses, making it highly addictive. Serotonin, GABA, glutamate, and dopamine are often the leading culprits in alcoholics' neurochemical imbalance. There are 22 or more types of serotonin, and you can inherit a low level, high level, or a normal level of each of these types. Of the twenty-two serotonins, some can be up, some down, some normal, and some not even there.

Why is knowledge of the existence of so many serotonin types so important? Because a lot of antidepressants will raise only certain serotonin subtypes. If it raises the serotonins that are already elevated and not the ones that are down, not only might the drug be rendered ineffective, it could also result in unappreciated side-effects. In all actuality, the practitioner is really guessing at which drugs are going to work. Patients have told me, "But the doctor said this would work on my depression!"

"Wow," I think to myself, "Does that doctor have a glass ball and a turban or what?'(Like Johnny Carson, if you remember that funny skit.) Right now there is no way of telling which of the serotonin subtypes are up or down in a patient's brain; there is no lab test to check that out. Sure we can do a brain biopsy, but that would be going too far. In cases of depression due to some sort of serotonin deficiency, the best bet is to pick a drug that will gently raise many serotonins. If you can find one that will hit the combination spot on, you are really going to get a great result without the side effects.

Furthermore, newer serotonin drugs have now been developed that specifically hit one serotonin subtype instead of multiple ones.

Experience tells us that the clues are there. We just have to take the time to listen and observe our patients carefully. It really works! Look at a patient's family history and take note of what drugs a person is self-medicating themselves with, and you will often learn what kind of deficiency they suffer from. Then you are well on your way to finding a solution.

Alcoholic Rats

Rats have long been used in research because they have similar diseases and problems to those of humans. Researchers wanted to verify the correlation that exists between low serotonin levels and alcoholism, so they put some rats to sleep and using very fine needles, penetrated the deep part of their limbic systems where the mid forebrain bundle lies. Using one needle, they perfused liquid into the brain and extracted some neurotransmitters through the other. They then measured each rat's serotonin levels and found that some rats had lower serotonin levels than others. Those with this serotonin deficiency, they called *B57 rats*.

Later on, they put both the B57 rats and the rats with normal levels of serotonin (normie rats) into cages that contained dishes of Vodka. Ostensibly, these B57 rats looked like any other rat in a rat cage. They had all the usual colors and ran around like all the other rats. However, if you were to look at their bellies, you would find a tattoo with something like "Harry B57" written on them. Never the less, once the dish of Vodka is in the cage, it suddenly became quite clear, even without looking at their bellies, which rats were the alcoholic ones. The normie rats would take one sniff or even taste and then keep away. Normal rats have sensitive noses, and the alcohol, which is toxic, burns their nostrils and is irritating to their stomachs. The B57 rats on the other hand, drank until they'd got slovenly drunk, developed big bellies, bit other rats, isolated themselves, and only wanted to drink (much like some humans do).

Clearly the mid forebrain bundle is where addiction is inherited. These B57 rats are alcoholic rats. They are alcoholic because they were born with a serotonin imbalance in their mid forebrain bundle. While the normie rats kept their distance from the nasty tasting vodka, the B57 rats indulged. A miraculous thing happened to the serotonin in the brains of the B57 rats when they drank the vodka: It went up into the low normal range. So now what did we have? A happy rat! (Or at least, a less depressed rat.) That is the reason why alcohol is considered an antidepressant. That antidepressant effect, however, does not last long because the bar closes at 2:00 a.m.

The Depressant Antidepressant

A bad thing will happen to serotonin levels if one drinks a lot and then stops drinking. Scientists discovered this problem in these B57 rats. When they eventually *did* stop drinking alcohol, their serotonin levels dropped even further below their genetic baseline. With serotonin levels lower than before they started drinking, they became even more depressed than they were naturally. This effect therefore indicates that alcohol is also a depressant. So alcohol has a two-fold effect. It initially acts as an antidepressant, but can ultimately cause depression. It takes three to four weeks for the severe drop in serotonin caused by heavy drinking to come back up to an individual's innate genetic level, thus the reason for the detoxification unit's 28- day program. Again, that restored innate level of neurotransmitters can be low compared with other people or rats, or it can be normal.

In a follow-up study, researchers gave the alcoholic B57 rats Prozac (which raises serotonin) and later put alcohol in the cage to see if the genetic alcoholic rats would still drink. After giving them the Prozac, the researchers measured the serotonin levels. They increased, but did not reach the level previously attained when given alcohol. The effect of alcohol is a great deal stronger; it raises serotonin much higher than even Prozac. Some people assumed that since Prozac raised the serotonin, the rats would not drink the

alcohol. Did they drink???

You bet they drank; they just drank less than when they were not on the Prozac. It appears that nothing compares to the effects and strength of alcohol.

The Powerful Drive to Feel (Better Than) Normal

If there is one thing that I have learned after working with over 20,000 drug addicts and alcoholics, it is that they *always* want to feel better than they feel at present, even when they are feeling "normal." I used to find it irritating when every morning, no matter what I did to help some of the alcoholics and drug addicts, when I went to the chemical dependency unit, there was a line of patients wanting to know how to feel better. Twenty years of dealing with that, and Prozac was looking pretty tempting.

It eventually occurred to me though, that these individuals are never satisfied with normality, and I finally figured out why. Prior to being addicted to anything, they sought out the substance that made them feel normal. This is the reason they do drugs and alcohol in the first place. Or perhaps they never even knew that the way they had been feeling their entire life was not in fact normal until one day they try something – a recreational drug, a prescription drug, or alcohol, and they suddenly feel like they can enjoy life the way it's meant to be. Whether they know it or not, they use the drugs and alcohol to raise certain neurotransmitter levels and reach a neurochemical balance which seems to them to be *normal*. Alcoholics and addicts are conditioned with every drink or pill they take to feel better because of some substance. They could be feeling great, but because of that incessant conditioned effect, they still want more than life will give them. Sure, one has to consider that they are depressed or in withdrawal or perhaps have some sort of pain issue; however, once their treatment ameliorates those symptoms, then that conditioned response of not being satisfied with normality creeps in.

Those rats on Prozac drank again because the alcohol had caused him or her to feel better every time, so why not hit it? But then again, the rat on Prozac drank less in quantity due to its improved neurotransmitter level. That leads us to the key to successful modern chemical dependency treatment: **Treat cravings by correcting the neurochemical imbalance.**

An Application of the Inquiry Method

In summary, when conducting an initial evaluation of someone, it is very important to examine the genetic characteristics of his or her family. You will find out things about your patient from a very objective perspective. Interestingly enough, patients can never diagnose themselves, but are quite good at diagnosing others. By gaining insight into my patients' genetic past, I can proceed to focus on them with questions pertaining to their moods, use of drugs, and things of that sort. Learning about an individual initially through the periphery of the family (for example grandparents) and then finally the patients themselves, I am able to discover things that I would not have normally been able to find out. First looking at the genetic profile and then inquiring as to what drugs they are currently taking and why, has proven most effective in obtaining clues regarding patients' neurochemical status and diagnosing the cause behind their drug dependency problems.

The other day I was sitting in front of a 32-year-old patient who had just lost his job. He suffers from depression and keeps a vodka bottle next to his bed. He lives in an apartment by himself and was drinking 24/7 before he came to this hospital. He told me that his fiancé was in his hospital room waiting to tell him their engagement was off. He had run out of his bipolar medications two weeks ago and within several days, started drinking. He avoided his fiancé naturally because of the shame of his downfall and relapse. He was crying, hyperventilating, trying to get up the courage, not to say he was sorry, but that he understood her feelings. After talking to me, he would face her and hear her words. I wondered what went wrong. Could just stopping the bipolar medications really have caused all of this?

I began my normal procedure of questioning. Soon I found out he was adopted and knew nothing about his birth parents. I questioned him, "you know nothing about them, *at all?" Nothing* was the answer. He had been taking Depakote, a GABA drug, along with a Serotonin medication. However, he said that he was getting progressive depression just prior to stopping these medications, meaning some neurochemical imbalance was progressive. "Probably not enough dopamine," I thought to myself. The man likely did not have enough D2. When thinking of possible ways to fix that, Abilify, a D2 drug, came to mind. A lot of bipolar and other depressed patients need that supercharge of dopamine added to the engine of serotonin.

Still the blank vacuum of his genetics haunted me. Were his genetic parents alcoholics? There was no way to know for certain, but there had to be some dopamine, noradrenergic, or glutamate problems in the genetic hardware of this man. With that, often comes alcoholism. It is a "chicken or egg" kind of circumstance, causing me to wonder: Do psychiatric disorders cause addiction, or does the addiction drive individuals into a DSM-IV psychiatric condition? They in fact dance with one another to the Blue Danube, feeding off of each other's movements.

Ultimately, I restarted his original GABA and Serotonin drugs and added Abilify to his list of prescribed medications. And his Fiancé? When we entered the room, she was crying. What that meant, I'm not sure, but I was hoping for the best for them both.

By taking a closer look into what neurochemical deficiencies are responsible for which cravings and diseases, as well as which medications and methods can be used to effectively treat people with those deficiencies, we can successfully treat people with drug dependency problems. It is my hope that by writing this book, it will serve as an aid to all those endeavoring to treat patients on their way to a lifelong recovery.

Brain Rules

Rule #9: The genetics we receive from our parents contain the instructions to how our brain and the neurotransmitter systems are formed. It is that formation that plays a huge role in determining our quality of life and susceptibility to alcoholism and drug abuse.

Rule #10: Each person is born with genetically determined levels of neurotransmitters. Some of us inherit an imbalance of these neurotransmitters or their receptors.

Rule #11: Psychiatric disease combined with illicit drug abuse creates a complex neurochemical derangement.

Rule #12: Underlying chemical imbalances are what lead to cravings for alcohol and drugs. If you treat the imbalance, you treat the cravings, and if you treat the cravings, you treat the addiction.

Rule #13: When conducting an initial evaluation of a chemically dependent patient, it is beneficial to first inquire about the patient's family history of alcoholism, drug abuse, and psychiatric disorders. Doing this provides deeper insight into what neurochemical imbalance(s) could possibly be behind their addiction.

"When anticipating the severity of the detoxification, it is vital for doctors to focus on the neurotransmitter imbalance. They must keep in mind that they are detoxifying the degree of the imbalance, not the amount of substance taken that caused that imbalance."

Chapter 5

Tolerance, Withdrawal, and Detoxification

The first day I ever felt *real* pain at 6 years old, was the day I decided to become a doctor. I came from humble beginnings, living in the middle of the Nevada desert, when one day I cut my head wide open and the local doctor tried to stitch me up using some worthless anesthesia. It hurt so bad, that I bit that doctor's hand until it bled. Needless to say, he kicked us out, and on the long stretch of road to the next doctor in Las Vegas, my dad asked me why I had to go ahead and bite the only doctor within a hundred miles. I tried to explain how much it hurt and told him not to worry because in the future I was going to be a doctor.

I hated pain then, and I hate it now. I have a deep respect for people suffering from pain and a clear understanding that people in pain need pain control. I also have enough experience in the field to know that there exist both responsible and detrimental methods of pain control. Today's most common methods of pain control often lead to tolerance. Tolerance, the diminution of response to some sort of substance, occurs because of extended use or prolonged exposure to that substance. The term *tolerance* is commonly used to explain one's built-up ability to resist the effect of either an illicit drug, or often alcohol. But the truth of the matter is, tolerance occurs for a number of different drugs, both illicit and prescribed – and where tolerance is, there is often addiction.

It is not uncommon to find patients with various kinds of chronic pain who have been placed on increasingly higher doses of narcotics over the years and now desire freedom from their dependence. When the patients attempt to taper off the medication themselves, they can no longer determine if they are experiencing true pain or rather the severe symptoms of withdrawal. Many times the patient will continue to have pain, and it must be addressed with methods other than using narcotics. It is the responsibility and moral imperative of doctors to find and use the best method possible, one that avoids the snares and maladies of tolerance.

Disabling Neurochemical Receptor Sites

Tolerance is a result of the habitual use of alcohol or other drugs such as Valium-type medications called benzodiazepines. Tolerance is an indicator of danger. It causes an individual to take ever-increasing amounts of a drug to get the desired effect. That increase means more molecules of the drug in the bloodstream hitting target receptors in the brain and periphery to get, in many cases, a pain-killing effect.

For years, the pharmaceutical industry has been trying to address this issue of tolerance and how it occurs, and we in the detoxification field have recently made some breakthroughs. We now have a new understanding as to just what is happening in the brain as tolerance increases. It is all tied to the receptor sites – the targets of the neurotransmitter systems in the brain that the molecules of drugs stimulate. When these target receptor sites are hit hard frequently with high doses of molecules, the neurological system essentially starts thinking that this is not a normal thing, thus causing the receptor sites to turn off, as if they were slowly disappearing over time. As the receptor sites start "disappearing," so does the effect of these molecules. The result is tolerance.

Swarming the Receptor Sites

Throughout history, a common strategy of military attack used during times of war was called *swarming*. The idea behind swarming would be to suddenly hit the enemy very hard at various targets all at once with tons of troops and then back away from the counter-attack. Subsequently, they would wait a day or two and then hit again with the same force. They would repeat this pattern over and over again until the enemy was severely crippled or running away. This was Napoleon's offense tactic.

Swarming the receptor sites of the brain with drugs, whether in the opiate centers or other neurotransmitter centers, produces much the same results. While increasing the dosage and frequency of whatever drug, the neurochemical receptor sites are essentially becoming disabled, as if they were no longer there. When the receptor sites throughout the brain and spinal cord experience this, we call it *down-regulation*.

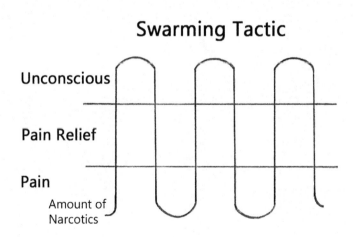

Much like the swarming tactic in war, repeatedly inundating receptor sites with excess molecules of drugs, whether illicit or prescribed, leads to the receptor sites' disablement and the patient's down-regulation.

The process of gaining tolerance mirrors the swarming tactic of war.

Down-regulation in the Hospital

People experience down-regulation of different neurotransmitter receptor sites depending on what drug and how much they use, and sadly it is occurring more and more with the use of opiates. Even more appalling, is the fact that it is highly preventable. Tolerance often occurs among patients who use various opiates such as morphine, codeine, Dilaudid, Demerol, Vicodin (or other forms of hydrocodone), fentanyl, or OxyContin, just to name a few. [9]

Many people who go to the hospital to get procedures done stay for a week or two. In order to insure that the patient does not experience any pain throughout the duration of their stay, the medical staff will administer frequent doses of intravenous high-volume opiates. Not only will this take care of the pain, it could also cause the patient to become somnolent and go to sleep. If large amounts are given, these frequent every two- or three-hour high-volume doses of opiates are in effect swarming the brain's opiate receptor sites, thereby increasing tolerance and leading some receptors to become disabled. These methods of administration clearly mirror the military tactic of swarming. After weeks or even months of this, if the dosage is high enough, the patient's brain will down-regulate. He or she will not get the same effect from the same concentration of molecules trying to hit the receptor sites. The receptor sites literally start to become dysfunctional after this period of extreme exposure. Therefore, the patient does not have the same pain control that he or she once had. That is tolerance.

Tolerance and Addiction

It is not uncommon for people to leave the hospital with a new addiction. Vicodin is a common culprit. Anyone taking over six Vicodin per day, at 5 mg hydrocodone, not only has a change

---

9 OxyContin and Percocet are both brand names for oxycodone, but Percocet also contains acetaminophen.

in the receptor sites, but also a suppression of his or her own beta-endorphin.[10] We know that six is the limit because we rarely see someone who needs detoxification taking less than five or six Vicodin a day. Is it fair to say that these people are addicted? Well, they would definitely go into physical withdrawal once the drug is terminated; therefore they have an increased amount of tolerance and are physically addicted to that drug.

It is amazing just how far tolerance can go. We have evaluated people who have an unlimited supply of Vicodin and are consuming it at an increasing rate over two or three years. Typically, a human being will max out due to the increased amount of tolerance and down-regulation. By the third year, some people are taking twenty, thirty, fifty, or even one hundred Vicodin pills per day. Clearly this is a significant increase in the molecular concentration of the hydrocodone or opiate surrounding the few receptor sites that remain functional. In addition to receptor sites becoming disabled, the patient's own production of beta-endorphin is severely suppressed.

Tolerance Begets Withdrawal

Once tolerance is developed and the drug is then discontinued, there has been a significant down-regulation of the neurochemical receptor sites, and the ones that remain functional are suddenly no longer being hit. That is when you have a new issue to contend with, and that issue is called *withdrawal*. Withdrawal symptoms are caused by an imbalance of neuroreceptors that are reactivating and returning to that person's original state. Being a painful process, it is as if the individual experiencing withdrawal is giving birth to zillions of these neuroreceptors. Drinking alcohol or taking drugs increases the amount of neurotransmitters released; halting those practices causes neurotransmitters to plummet. A neurochemical imbalance of the brain and the receptor sites has been created, and withdrawal is the resulting condition. The next step now is detoxi-

---

10 Beta-endorphin is the body's endogenous morphine.

fication, which can get precarious with all this neural activity going on. Our job as doctors and nurses is to assist the patient's brain in safely returning to its natural equilibrium.

Throughout the detoxification process, physicians and nurses monitor the progress of their patients according to a timetable, which is set out in what we refer to as *the detoxification curve*. The detoxification curve outlines what is happening to the brain's neurotransmitters with the passage of time. Manifestations of

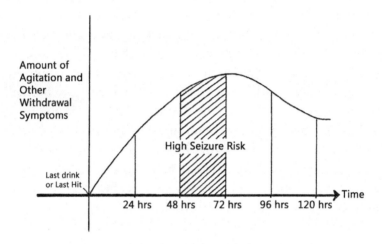

The Detoxification Curve

withdrawal peak approximately 72 hours after the patient last used alcohol or the other abused substance. Medications administered to patients to ameliorate the harsh symptoms of withdrawal, like agitation, tremulousness, and so forth, also peak at this point. This is considered the top of the curve. It is during the interval of 48 to 72 hours that seizure activity would normally take place because the brain is racing at its fastest (especially for those recovering from alcohol and benzodiazepines). We prevent that from occurring by balancing their high agitating glutamate with equally high doses of tranquilizing GABA drugs. It seems that the brain finds somewhat of a balance after the first 72 hours. Once the patient has passed the 72-hour peak of the curve and is going down its slope, we administer less medication because the brain is then up-regulating at a safer speed.

Detoxification – The Process of Up-Regulation

How a patient responds to the detoxification process is not dependent on the length of time, nor the amount of drug that the person has used. While the dosage (amount and frequency) of drugs has determined the extent of the changes in receptor sites (tolerance), it does not determine the severity of the symptoms of the withdrawal. Rather, the receptor sites returning to normality (up-regulation) determines the severity. Why? The reason for this is there is a maximum amount of suppression. At some point, due to tolerance, it does not matter how many molecules of the drug you are putting into your blood stream because there is only a limited amount of receptors available to be hit. So tolerance has a limit or a "T-max." *T-max* refers to the verity that with any type of reaction, there are limiting factors or elements where the reaction will max out. For example, consider someone who mixes together a substrate and a catalyst to form a new compound. By limiting the amount of either one of those elements, there is a limiting factor in how much product will be made. The same is true with the limited amount of working receptors.

Picture a wall with five holes in it. The holes are the receptor sites, and ping-pong balls represent molecules of drugs that supplement the natural activity of neurotransmitters. If you have five ping-pong balls to hit those holes you have a good reaction. Now leave the five ping-pong balls, but (to represent the kind of tolerance that occurs after swarming) eliminate four of the holes so only one remains. All those ping-pong balls are bouncing around in the area with only one hole available, and few actual hits oc-curring. Thus, no matter how many molecules of, let's say opiates, are hitting the receptor sites, there are only a limited number of receptor sites being activated. This is true for any neurotransmit-ter receptors' change that results from extreme benzodiazepine, alcohol, or other drug use.

The severity of withdrawal and detoxification is dependent upon how many receptors remain functional and capable of being hit by molecules of the drug. Down-regulation of neurotransmitter receptor sites occur because the unnatural, abusive hyper-activity at the target sites caused them to shut down, so to speak, causing the whole system to adjust to a new, seemingly reasonable balance. Where before there were myriads of active functional receptor sites, after down-regulating, there now exist only a few, thus the imbalance is in place. If the new imbalance is only minor, then the detoxifica-tion will be mild, but if a marked degree of receptor inhibition has transpired, then the magnitude of the detoxification will be greater. When anticipating the severity of the detoxification, it is vital for doctors to focus on the neurotransmitter imbalance. They must keep in mind that they are detoxifying the degree of the imbalance, not the amount of substance taken that caused that imbalance.

Consider the example of detoxifying someone off of OxyCon-tin. When a person goes into detoxification by removing all of the OxyContin, how much of it has been taken does not matter. For instance, I treated a patient who was taking ten 80mg tablets of OxyContin a day, and he was worried he was going to experience worse detoxification symptoms than someone taking only four or five. I explained to him that if someone were taking one hundred 80mg tablets of OxyContin, the detoxification would be the same. It is the receptor sites coming back into normality that determines the severity of the detoxification, not the amount of OxyContin one has taken nor over what time interval.

Once someone has gone off of opiate-based drugs and detoxi-fied, receptor sites are re-activated, the beta-endorphin kicks in

There is a limit to the amount of tolerance that can be built up from drug or alcohol abuse. At some point, it does not matter how many molecules of the drug are in the blood stream because due to down-regulation, there is only a limited amount of receptor sites available for stimulation.

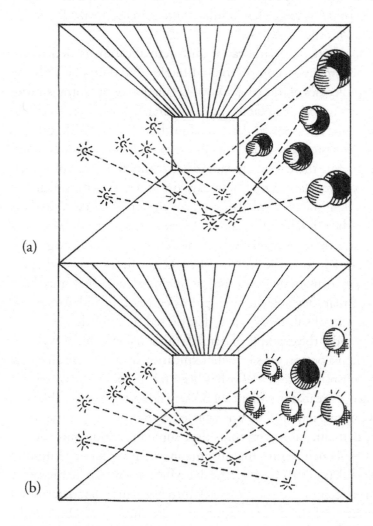

(a) Before tolerance is built, there are plenty of receptor sites available for stimulation, reacting to neurotransmitters and molecules of drugs.
(b) After tolerance is built and down-regulation has occurred, there is a limited amount of receptor sites available to be stimulated.

again, and it seems that the result is better pain control. In thousands of detoxifications of patients with back surgeries who have maxed out on high-dose narcotics, 90 percent of them have better pain control because their receptor sites have been successfully reactivated. In addition, their beta-endorphin has kicked in, and we are using other methods of pain management. There are many other non-opiate methods of pain management that responsible doctors can employ. One option is to use non-steroidal anti-inflammatory medications that will reduce firing of nerves, such as gabapentin (Neurontin), Lyrica, and Lidoderm patches. There are also newer noradrenergic-based medications, like Cymbalta, Effexor, and Savella, which block pain impulses from both the spine and lower body. It is essential to treat all underlying diseases and make sure all surgeries and epidurals are done prior to detoxifying patients, so as not to tamper with their neurochemistry more than once.

The Danger of Going Back

Once a person is successfully detoxified, that person's receptor sites have become up-regulated, and the high tolerance that he or she once possessed, no longer exists. Given that all the receptor sites are fully functional again, if that person takes the same amount of drugs or narcotics that he had previously been taking, there is a high probability that he will overdose and die. Unfortunately, this kind of situation occurs often and is common with fentanyl, namely Duragesic. However, if the former addict does survive the initial stage of relapse, within several days the whole system will down-regulate again, and all the receptor sites that were once disabled, will return to that non-functional state. The level of down-regulation that it took months or even years to initially reach will now occur within mere days. The receptor sites have a memory like an elephant; they will down-regulate every time for the rest of one's life.

Contrary to what many believe, this is a huge problem that could possibly affect the lives of anyone – not just drug addicts.

Due to the wiles of tolerance and the increase in the availability of narcotics in the United States today (especially so with OxyContin) we are facing an epidemic. People's neurotransmitter systems are being permanently damaged by the over-prescription of narcotics. Laws that have pressured those in the medical profession to use narcotics at higher and higher doses have added to the incidence of this issue. Law firms with the support of the Pharmaceutical Industry have done their utmost to make sure that M.D.s give pain medications to anyone in pain. In California, the California Pain Act set forth laws that increased the number of prescriptions for narcotics. So it goes, too much of a good thing can in fact be a bad thing.

A few years ago, the President of the California Society of Addiction Medicine published an article about the concerns associated with the increased use of narcotics at all levels. At that time, there was a high incidence of overdose and death caused by OxyContin. Young people everywhere were, and still are, affected adversely by this and other opiate-based medications. This concern is very real and there are moral and ethical issues surrounding it. I have detoxified 10,000 patients off opiates over the past 30 years, many of which had a high incidence of repeat surgeries. Within several days of taking the narcotics to cope with the pain from surgery, these patients completely down-regulated and immediately went into withdrawal once the medications were discontinued. Certainly, I can attest to the weightiness of this issue.

It is a disturbing truth that the young people who have taken enough opiate pain medications to down-regulate their opiate systems once, will have an injury to their neurotransmitter systems that will last a lifetime. Many people fail to realize that we only get one set of neurotransmitter systems. Once an individual has used high dose narcotics for an extended period of time and the neurotransmitter system has down-regulated, that person's brain will forever recall that tolerance for the rest of his or her life. So what's the big deal? As long as they get off the drugs or medication, they can lead healthy, normal lives, right? Not quite.

We should refrain from being so short-sighted. If we destroy our opiate system by placing a conditioned memory in our body's natural coping mechanism for pain while we are young, we will be ill-prepared to deal with the aches and pains incidental to aging. The older we get, the more we need pain control. If people burn up their one set of neurotransmitters when they are young, they will likely spend the rest of their life with pain control problems. Personally, I am deeply upset and very angered at what has happened to young people's opiate systems due to this miscalculation and marketing of drugs and the laws that have driven this silent injustice.

Brain Rules

Rule #14: Tolerance is caused by receptor site modification and other complex neurochemical changes.

Rule #15: Withdrawal is the resulting condition when a neurochemical imbalance of the brain and the receptor sites has been created because of alcohol or drug abuse.

Rule #16: Detoxification from drugs or alcohol is pretty much the process of the neurotransmitter imbalances up-regulating, returning to their genetically endowed levels.

Rule #17: The severity of a detoxification is dependent upon how many receptors are left to be activated and on the degree of the neurotransmitter imbalance, not on the quantity of drug last consumed.

Rule #18: You are not detoxifying the amount of narcotic, benzodiazepine, alcohol, or any other drug – illicit or prescribed; you are detoxifying the changes or damage done to the affected receptor sites in the brain.

Rule #19: Once an individual's neurotransmitter system has down-regulated, the level of down-regulation that it took months or even years of drug abuse to reach initially, will now occur within mere days (assuming the person even survives the initial relapse).

"When it comes to alcohol and drug abuse, sometimes our actions are dictated purely by choice and other times we are driven by a physiological deficiency."

Chapter 6

Nature *and* Nurture

The debate of nature versus nurture has seeped into virtually all areas of life. The question remains, how much of how we feel, what we do, and basically who we are, is passed on to us by our parents and how much is shaped by our experiences and environment? The truth is they both play a role. For instance, a neurochemical imbalance can be self-induced or someone can be born with it. When it comes to alcohol and drug abuse, sometimes our actions are dictated purely by choice and other times we are driven by a physiological deficiency.

As brought out in chapter 4, the twenty-three chromosomes we receive from each parent contain the instructions to how our brain and the neurotransmitter systems within it are formed. It is that formation that plays a huge role in determining our quality of life. Not only are these powerful neurotransmitters linked to our inclination towards addiction, they also play a role in shaping our personalities, how we feel, and how we interpret the world around us.

Neurotransmitters and Personality

The way the brain is organized, as well as its balance of neurotransmitters and their interactions with one another, are highly influential in determining our actions and the reasoning behind them. As mentioned earlier, the brain works like a computer with a central processing unit (CPU), our mid forebrain bundle, in the middle. Genetics essentially determine the quality of this neurochemical hardware, which in turn runs our environmental software. The temporal lobe is like a disk, where the information we learn is imprinted. Everything we learn through education, family, consequences, and trial and error is stored in these temporal lobes. In turn, what we learn helps shape who we are.

Additional defining factors in our personality are (1) how we interpret and interact with the world around us and (2) self-perception, which is revealed through thought and motivation. We learn morals, ethics, and social boundaries through our upbringing and throughout our lives' experiences with various people in a plethora of different situations. How we react to those social boundaries and mores contribute to the kind of people we become. But those reactions are heavily dependent on how we *process* the incoming information. Furthermore, how we process that information is largely determined by the hardware we are born with.

How, if the brain is so dynamic and tremendously vast in its functions, does it compare with a computer? The answer lies within how the brain processes information. The CPU of a computer typically will organize or pull things off of software in a standard way. Like the hardware of a computer, the brain may have an abnormality, which causes it to assemble information from the various senses in an unusual way (different than an average person's brain would). It might even focus on different data all together, data that a typical person would not even pay attention to. This can result from a neurochemical imbalance, the kind that afflicts various people of all levels of intelligence. There are accomplished people out there who have this kind of neurochemical and processing deficiency, but life experience has taught them how to conceal this difference by constantly keeping themselves in check so others do not suspect something is amiss. The information which has been filtered and altered in some way is stored for future use in the brain's memory bank – the temporal lobe. Once this abnormally processed information is placed in the brain's data bank, any time it is retrieved or called to mind, the memory, along with the reasoning surrounding it, may come out a great deal different than the average person's would.

Like a computer, how we process information is fundamental in determining how we function. It is our neurochemicals that determine how our brain processes the world around us, in turn

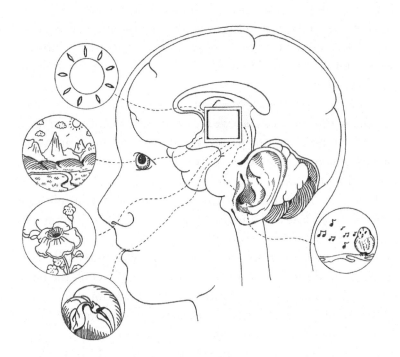

Information in all forms, after being received through the senses, is then processed through our brain's CPU, the mid forebrain bundle. The way we process our environment is dependent on the neurochemical hardware we are born with.

shaping our personalities. We inherit these neurotransmitters at certain levels due to genetics; however there are other factors that can modify them. They are always trying to find their balance, yet this balance can be compromised and challenged daily by various factors such as hormones, environment, drugs, alcohol, and prescription medications.

Harnessing the Power of Neurotransmitters

Clearly both internal and external forces shape the very fiber of who we are. Interestingly enough though, there is no research out there that explains scientifically how exactly one's memories and environment form our personality. It is unknown what precisely happens within our mid forebrain bundle (the human CPU) or how memories are retrieved from the temporal lobe and then associated with one's current environment to develop personality. However, what is known and well researched is the effect that neurotransmitters have on our personalities.

How we view the world around us is a vital aspect of personality, and neurotransmitters have the power to influence that outlook on life. By utilizing this power and prescribing medications that improve patients' outlook, we can help them eliminate cravings and maintain sobriety. Take for example serotonin. Recent research indicates that drugs that are selective serotonin reuptake inhibitors, such as Prozac, can change the neurochemicals in a supposedly positive way, actually altering one's personality. By raising a person's serotonin, their brain forms more positive thoughts, making the world around them appear a great deal better. Overall, the person becomes much happier. We utilize this phenomenon to keep patients sober and off of other medications they were previously addicted to. Time and time again we have seen how proper use of neurotransmitter agonists can alter neurochemicals for the better, changing people's lives and in some cases granting them the basic will to continue living.

Essentially we are changing the way the patient's brain processes everything. By creating a new balance of neurotransmitters, prescribing the proper neurotransmitter agonists has the power to correct things like compulsiveness, neuroticism, and even severe cases of introversion. These methods also work to alleviate various symptoms of depression, such as extreme negativity and unnecessary guilt. By adjusting patients' neurotransmitter balances using the right medications, we can increase patients' ability to focus and to more accurately and better comprehend their environment. Once they associate the environment with the positive aspects of what they perceive, they can then know how to respond confidently and optimistically, acting upon those thoughts and the environment in a way that better sustains themselves and others. Positively altering how people perceive and interact with the world around them improves patients' quality of life, creating a day that has affirmative aspects to it, so that another day can follow.

Depression and Alcoholism

Depression is more than just an inability to cope with the sorrows of life. In most cases, its root cause is genetic. Research on the brain's activity during depression is flourishing. The prefrontal cortex is one of the areas of the brain that is particularly affected by depression, showing abnormally low activity. Recent studies conducted by PJ Fitzgerald and published in PubMed, revealed a well-supported hypothesis that the serotonin and noradrenaline systems (and the drugs that affect them) seem to work like on and off switches to the prefrontal cortex. Serotonin seems to activate the prefrontal cortex, and noradrenaline deactivates this region of the brain. Severely altering one's personality, depression is an ailment that can take over a person's life. In many ways, depression is a means of isolation. It causes extreme feelings of guilt and introversion because of a diminished ability to relate with surrounding people. Regrettably, depression often goes hand in hand with alcoholism because alcohol raises the neurotransmitters that medically depressed people are inherently low in.

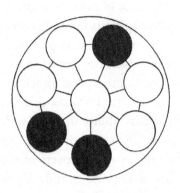

There are three neurotransmitter systems to consider when helping a patient to battle depression: serotonin, dopamine, and noradrenaline. People with severe depression often have genetic imbalances within one or more of these systems.

Fortunately, we do have medications to alleviate most cases of depression. What is of concern however, are the severest cases of depressed patients, the ones who have family histories of depression and suicide. For instance, one of my patients is a 38-year-old professional businessman whose mother committed suicide. While struggling to maintain both a marriage and a business, he drinks a fifth of hard liquor a day. With pressures increasing, we have attempted to detoxify him on two different occasions and failed. Using Ativan, a GABA drug, and serotonergic drugs, we have attempted to correct his neurochemical imbalance. However, when he starts detoxifying into the depths of the dopamine system and his opiates decrease due to the lack of alcohol, he is faced with a deeper depression evocative of the genetic tendency towards suicide.

I have often wondered why we cannot detoxify these kinds of patients. Their craving for alcohol is just too immense. Most are blackout drinkers, with blood alcohol levels approaching .300 BAC when they drink. These high levels cause the extremely addictive release of opiates and dopamine, both of which are miraculous antidepressants. These severely depressed individuals cannot tolerate the deeper type of depression that alcohol momentarily medicates. There must be a dopamine, noradrenaline, or some other serotonin problem that our medications simply aren't addressing when we try to detoxify them. The depression these patients experience is so overwhelming, they need alcohol to pull themselves out of this marked decline of detoxification before they crash. Understanding this is paramount.

Why people continue to drink when they have a family history of suicide or major depression has to be considered when contemplating treatment. The routines of typical physicians, psychiatrists, or detoxification units of simply placing the patient on a normal detoxification protocol and hoping for the best, does carry a high risk. If these patients do detoxify, the abyss of depression lies below and can result in a catastrophic outcome. One has to understand the neurotransmitter systems and try to use non-addictive medications that will support those neurotransmitter systems to assist them through the detoxification process and to keep the patient out of the landslide of depression and ensuing relapse.

For the above mentioned case, we tried to hit the serotonin receptors hard with antidepressant medications and D2 drugs such as Abilify or Wellbutrin, while also stabilizing GABA and glutamate. We also tried blocking the opiate system quickly using all parameters to try to get the patient to detoxify and nullify the underlying marked neurotransmitter inadequacies of depression. Blocking the opiate system in the nucleus accumbens with opiate receptor blockers (such as naltrexone, Narcan, and/or Vivitrol) is a very effective method when treating alcoholism by reducing cravings. It does so by also preventing the release of dopamine in the nucleus accumbens. The full effects of this dopamine release with regards to depression are still uncertain. It is clear though that rarely will you find someone taking opiates who is moderately or severely depressed. This is because of opiates' effect on the other neurotransmitter systems, especially on dopamine. The opiate system is like the Godfather of the brain; it rules with an iron hand, having a powerful influence on all the other neurochemical systems. When you remove the Godfather from the picture by getting someone off opiates, the power plays that occur among the remaining neurotransmitter systems are anyone's guess. That is what is so fascinating about getting a person off opiates who has been on them for years. Unfortunately the majority will never find out their true personality because for one reason or another, they will remain on high dose narcotics for the rest of their lives.

Long-Term Treatment of Genetic Imbalances

The first step to each detoxification, like any challenge you face, is to determine the source of the problem. After deciphering which substance caused the down-regulation of the neurotransmitters, it is of the utmost importance to probe into what led to the substance abuse in the first place. Is the neurotransmitter imbalance completely self-induced, or was the patient unknowingly attempting to self-medicate some sort of inherent deficiency? The answer to this question will determine the kind of care necessary, as well as the length of time required for the patient to take anti-craving medications.

Inherited neurotransmitter balances are a part of our brain's hardware. Like the hardware of a computer, it remains constant. But the software (anything introduced to the brain from our environment, like memories and lessons) is subject to change. The software that is placed in the computer will be altered significantly if the hardware has an abnormal electronic system or structure. If someone purchases a computer with a certain problem, it will process that problem the same way for as long as that person owns that computer. Hence, when the brain has a permanent abnormality or imbalance of different neurotransmitters, that problem will always be there, leading to certain cravings, habits, or abnormal ways of neurological processing.

People ask, "How long do I need to take the medication if my systems were genetically out of balance in the first place?" The answer to that lies within the way that individual's brain was genetically formed. If the chromosomes endowed by one's parents make the hardware part of the brain – including the neurotransmitters and their connections, then the design of those parts would be permanent. When there is an innate neurochemical imbalance, the source of the problem is in the structure of the brain, therefore these abnormalities are chronic, and will last a lifetime.

Genetic alcoholics and drug addicts use substances their entire adult lives to momentarily bring their neurotransmitters to higher levels, providing relief from their genetic deficiency of these essential mood modifiers. So how long should someone take anti-craving medications? It is evident that treating inherited neurochemical imbalances is a lifelong process. These neurotransmitter-deficient people need to take anti-craving medication for the rest of their lives in order to keep their neurotransmitter systems in proper balance. Many pharmaceutical companies have been evaluating drugs for anti-craving features for over five years now. The test results for these drugs that increase neurotransmitters are positive. They have seen two or three times less relapses of both drug and alcohol abuse.

The only exception to life-long treatment of neurochemical imbalances is when someone is drinking alcohol or taking cocaine, methamphetamine, or other drugs and has completely self-induced the neurotransmitter imbalance. In those cases, neurotransmitters will go back to healthy normal levels in three to four weeks (sometimes longer, especially in cases of methamphetamine use). It is a critical time during those three to four weeks to determine whether the imbalance is genetic or self-induced. Cravings are more likely to go away if the imbalance is not genetic.

If nothing is done to decrease further cravings for those with genetic deficiencies, throughout the fourth, fifth, or sixth week, one can relapse. It takes wisdom and vigilance on the part of the patient's physician, family, and spouse to be aware of what may or may not be signs of cravings. A person's neural hardware lasts for a lifetime. If a patient does not take the prescribed anti-craving medicine that he or she needs, the patient will seek the drug of choice to satisfy the neurochemical imbalance bequeathed to them through genetics.

Brain Rules

Rule #20: An individual's brain may have a neurochemical imbalance that causes the brain to assemble information from the various senses in an unusual way. Once this abnormally processed information is placed in the brain's temporal lobe, any time the information is retrieved, the memory and the reasoning surrounding it may come out different than the average person's would.

Rule #21: Our neurochemical balances determine how our brain processes the world around us. How our brain processes this information is fundamental in shaping our personalities and determining how we function.

Rule #22: How an individual's brain processes and interprets information is also subject to the influence of various factors such as hormones, environment, drugs, alcohol, and prescription medications.

Rule #23: Neurotransmitters influence our outlook on life; by utilizing this power and prescribing medications that improve patients' outlook, we can help them to maintain sobriety by eliminating their cravings.

Rule #24: By adjusting a patient's balance of neurotransmitters, we are essentially changing the way the patient's brain processes everything. When done properly, this can alleviate things like depression, compulsiveness, neuroticism, and cravings.

Rule #25: To avoid a catastrophic outcome when detoxifying severely depressed suicidal patients, treatment *must* go beyond normal protocol and non-addictive medications that support their deficient neurotransmitter systems must be used.

Rule #26: When the brain has a genetic abnormality or neurotransmitter imbalance, that problem will always be there, leading to

certain cravings, habits, or abnormal ways of neurological processing, unless continually corrected with the proper neurochemical-
adjusting medications.

Rule #27: It is vital to ascertain the source of patients' neurochemical imbalance. Establishing whether it started off as an inherited
imbalance or if it is strictly self-induced with alcohol or drug abuse,
will determine the kind of treatment each patient needs – whether
it will be short-term, or life-long.

Rule #28: If the initial source of the neurochemical imbalance
is genetic, it will be necessary for the patient to take anti-craving
or psychiatric medication for the rest of his or her life to prevent
relapse.

"Alcohol is the ultimate stimulant for the brain. … It moves the brain's neurochemicals like no other drug on the planet. … All this stimulation makes alcohol a powerful anti-depressant … and an even more powerful depressant once it wears off."

Chapter 7

The Power of
Alcohol and Nicotine

Of all the drugs known to man, there is only one capable of raising five, sometimes six, of the eight neurotransmitters that shape the way we experience life. That drug is alcohol. We in the detoxification profession refer to it as *the mother of all drugs* or *the kick-ass drug*. The pharmaceutical industry has never produced a drug as all encompassing in its effect as alcohol.

Most drugs will raise one or two neurotransmitters at a time. Often antidepressant medications will raise serotonin and possibly a little noradrenaline. It is rare to find pharmaceutical agents that will raise two or three neurochemical systems. Wellbutrin (bupropion), the most powerful pharmaceutical agent out there, is an antidepressant medication that will actually raise three in somewhat of a reasonable manner: noradrenaline, dopamine, and acetylcholine.

Alcohol is the ultimate stimulant for the brain. To date, we know of no other agent that comes close to matching its power; alcohol's effect on the human body is unprecedented. This influential drug is ultra-powerful as a neurotransmitter agonist. It moves the brain's neurochemicals like no other drug on the planet. Alcohol raises serotonin, GABA, endocannabinoid, glutamate, and at high dose, increases the release of opiates. It also has a significant end-result effect on dopamine (which is very euphoric), adding up to a total of six neurotransmitters being affected. All this stimulation makes alcohol a powerful anti-depressant (not to mention highly addictive) and an even more powerful depressant once it wears off, causing neurotransmitters to plummet.

The Most Powerful Drug and its Accomplice

If you ever attend an Alcoholics Anonymous (AA) meeting or a Narcotics Anonymous (NA) meeting, you will find plenty of coffee and many people smoking cigarettes on every break they get. It has been that way for thirty or forty years. Many people, including practitioners and therapists, do not understand the association of nicotine with alcohol in chemical dependency treatment. Most observers assume that the heavy presence of coffee and cigarettes indicates that there is something wrong with these people. Perhaps, they assume, these people have "addictive personalities" and though they have given up alcohol, still need to hang onto some vice – caffeine or nicotine. However, once one understands how the eight interconnected neurotransmitters systems work and know that their inherited deficiencies are what lead to predisposition to addiction problems, it becomes evident that the real underlying problem has nothing to do with some obscure personality flaw.

Alcohol's strong effect on five of the eight neurotransmitter systems just so happens to be complimented perfectly by nicotine, a strong stimulant of the remaining three – acetylcholine, noradrenaline, and dopamine. When one adds up the agonistic or positive stimulating effects of both alcohol and nicotine, one has eight different systems that are all strongly being affected. Now imagine trying to get alcoholics to quit smoking while at the same time stop drinking.

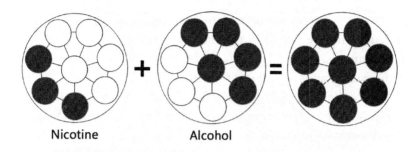

Nicotine   Alcohol

The combined effects of alcohol and nicotine use result in the powerful stimulation of all eight of the neurotransmitter systems. No wonder people have a
hard time quitting cigarettes and alcohol at the same time!

Many chemical dependency treatment centers ban the use of
both alcohol and nicotine while their patients are in the program.
That is quite a hit to the patients. Some people can do it; some
cannot. When a patient has eight neurochemical systems that are
suddenly not being stimulated due to detoxification, that body is
going to experience quite a bit of withdrawal. It is therefore un-
derstandable why so many of these patients latch onto nicotine.
Letting go of five neurotransmitters as oppose to all eight, makes
the withdrawal process slightly more bearable.

I am by no means condoning the use of nicotine. Nicotine is
a dangerous drug, to say the least. It sends countless numbers of
people to the hospital and kills 300,000 people a year. I merely
wish to shed some light on the concept of alcohol and nicotine
treatment, that way an understanding can be had of what occurs
on a neurochemical basis when a patient halts the use of both of
these drugs.

Nicotine and Acetylcholine

Acetylcholine is one of the neurotransmitter systems that are
associated with nicotinic acetylcholine receptors (nAChR). There

has been a lot of research on nicotine receptor mechanisms. There are twelve subtypes of the nAChRs within this neurotransmitter system. They are found in the thalamus, the cerebral cortex, the hippocampus, the basal ganglia, and the cerebellum. Acetylcholine is the endogenous ligand of this system.

Once the bindings of these nAChR receptor sites occur, there is a subsequent release of norepinephrine (NE), serotonin (5-HT), and dopamine (DA). It is believed opiate peptides are also released. Hence the nicotinic acetylcholine receptors are responsible for many neurochemical activations. There are a lot of alcoholics who smoke cigarettes due to the multiple neurotransmitters that are affected by the drug. As with the other neurotransmitter systems, tolerance eventually occurs. If one increases their intake of nicotine, soon the receptor sites down-regulate, becoming disabled or inactive, thus requiring more and more nicotine to get the desired effect.

Recent studies help us to understand why nicotine addiction is so powerful and prevalent in our society. Cigarette users experience many positive effects, such as improvement in cognition and cognitive associations, as well as an increased amount of working memory. Individuals who have difficulty concentrating, experience improvement in their concentration. Benefits also extend to those suffering from mental illness. Schizophrenics experience an increase in memory, and bipolar patients experience an enhanced mood. Smoking to some extent improves depression through the subsequent dopamine and serotonin release that occurs with nAChR receptor site stimulation. One can clearly see by looking at the effects of nicotine on the neurotransmitter systems, why it is so difficult to stop drinking *and* smoking.

Quitting the Nicotine

By raising dopamine and noradrenaline, nicotine has an antidepressant effect. Suicidal thoughts and severe depression is not uncommon among patients who cut off their nicotine intake completely. Nevertheless, this is not an excuse to continue smoking. In fact, there are drugs out there that can combat some of the detrimental effects of nicotine withdrawal. Wellbutrin may be an adjunct for this depression. It has been known to increase some of the neurotransmitters that nicotine also stimulates. Additionally, Zyban and another drug called Chantix both hit the alpha4beta2 receptor sites on cells, which have an effect similar to nicotine, without all the bad consequences.

Why We Drink and Cannot Stop

Craving is merely a neurotransmitter imbalance. In this setting, *imbalance* typically means the individual has a low amount of either one or several neurotransmitter types. I have often reasoned to myself that it is not that alcoholics inherit alcoholism, but more specifically they inherit a state of brain function that lacks the proper amount of neurochemicals, the amount that the average non-alcoholic mind enjoys. Alcohol momentarily alleviates that insufficiency by raising five or six of these neurochemicals.

Which of the five or six neurochemicals are out of balance varies from person to person, as well as how many different neurochemicals they are short on. Since alcohol raises a number of neurochemicals, it is ambiguous as to which ones are really in need of being satisfied for each individual. The disparity of each one also varies according to each individual's brain chemical make-up. No matter which neurotransmitter(s) the individual is short on, he or she will seek to maximize the elevation of those neurotransmitters with alcohol so they can feel better or "normal." The cravings these genetic alcoholics feel, if unremedied, can lead to impulsive alcohol or drug use. The result of this can be not only physical, but also conditional, increasing the likelihood that the practice will be repeated due to the intensified satisfaction of the reward.

We know that alcohol is a tremendously effective drug for our neurotransmitters and that is why it is so difficult to quit. The only thing more powerful than alcohol's antidepressant effects is its depressant effects. Within a day or two of quitting alcohol, a person's neurotransmitters suddenly drop, falling below their genetically inherited levels. At this point the individual is depressed for several weeks until their neurochemical balance finally returns to that person's normal levels. The brain's up-regulation (its returning to its natural chemical balance) is what detoxification is all about. It returns to its natural balance after three or four weeks. Thus the reason for so many 28-day programs throughout the United States.

The Magic of 28 Days

For years we have known that something amazing happened after 28 days of treatment. While in these detoxification programs where their neurochemicals are allowed to come into proper balance, patients are introduced to the principles and concepts of the need for sobriety. They are also reminded of past consequences of their drug and alcohol use and educated on their future life of sobriety. If for that period of time patients successfully stay away from alcohol, not only are they be markedly healthier and happier, they also wake up with self-recognition, new goals, and new relationships.

The Old Method of Treatment

In detoxifications we are not just dealing with people, we are dealing with these very powerful neurochemicals. For years counselors have made the mistake of using the act of drinking alcohol as the decisive factor in determining the failure or effectiveness of treatment. They would ask their alcoholic patients, "Did you drink since I have seen you last?" Unfortunately, if the answer was yes, that act of drinking could have immediately lead to major complications or losses concerning family, jobs, legal actions, depression, financial issues, or even hospitalization. Therefore we can no longer stick to this old method of perceiving the event of drinking as the factor of success because by the time the counselor or doctor finds out that the patient did drink or use drugs again, the damage is already done. We must be more aggressive in our treatment. We must solve the problem *before* it becomes a bigger problem, not after, thereby avoiding the devastation of relapse.

The New Method of Treatment:
Focus on the Cravings

Modern techniques use craving as the new indicator of neu-rotransmitter imbalances and as a warning sign of heavy drinking and drug use. Now we ask them, "Are you craving alcohol or any other drug of your choice?" Cravings can be displayed in many ways: from just wanting a drink, to anger, impatience, hostility, anxiety, dysphoria, and any other demeanor characteristic of that individual before they drink or use drugs. In my clinical practice, I look at these cravings to determine which medications can best alleviate each individual's neurochemical imbalances.

The goal in the modern treatment of alcoholics is to achieve a state of "no cravings" through the use of medications that remedy the neurochemical imbalances. Smart and effective treatment lies within this new method of relapse prevention, as oppose to the old method of trying to fix the situation after the catastrophic events and devastation of relapse occurs. We will talk about the effective-ness of modern medications and how to use them next.

Brain Rules

Rule #29: Alcohol is the ultimate stimulant for the brain. It raises serotonin, GABA, endocannabinoid, glutamate, and at high dose, increases the release of opiates and dopamine, adding up to a total of six neurotransmitters. When referring to these six neurotransmitter systems affected by alcohol, I call them the *alcohol system*.

Rule #30: Combining the effects of alcohol and nicotine results in the strong stimulation and elevation of *all* of the eight basic neurotransmitter systems.

Rule #31: The key objective of modern alcohol treatment is to achieve a state of "no cravings" through the use of medications and treatment, thereby avoiding the pitfalls of relapse.

"Detoxification treatment is all about getting the patient's neurotransmitters back to their normal genetic state as safely as possible."

Chapter 8

Treating Alcoholics

Detoxifying alcoholic patients off alcohol is only the first 5 percent of their treatment. To get an alcoholic to stop drinking, it takes a lot more than just that first step of detoxification. Patients need a treatment plan, education, and continued monitoring in recovery. In addition, they require the necessary medications to stop their cravings. Anti-craving medications are aimed at alleviating the symptoms associated with low levels of the six neurotransmitters that are momentarily raised by alcohol.

Addressing Underlying Problems

When treating alcoholics and patients with other addiction problems, it is important to always seek out the underlying problem, as well as consider any possible psychiatric disorders they might be suffering from. Remember, if the patient is bipolar or has some other psychiatric diagnosis and the psychiatric disorder goes untreated, altering their alcohol-effected neurotransmitters will not ensure success. Cases dealing with these particular kinds of situations will be covered with greater detail in future chapters and case studies.

A strong correlation exists between opiate addiction and alcoholism. Every day I take care of patients who are addicted to opiates, and it is never surprising to find that beneath the veneer of "opiate addict," is an actual genetic alcoholic. Often opiate addicts have one or two parents who are alcoholic. Why the strong correlation? This relationship exists for two reasons: (1) alcohol acts as an agonist to the opiate system in the nucleus accumbens, and (2) alcohol activates almost the entire system of neurotransmitter groups which each have tight communication ties to the opiate system. For the most effective treatment, it is important to remember that more often than not, your opiate-addicted patients are really genetic alcoholics. That subject will be covered in more depth later, but for now, I will just provide some simple pointers on the drugs and methods I do and do not use for treating alcoholics most of the time.

GABA versus Glutamate

Alcohol is an incredibly strong neurotransmitter agonist that raises neurotransmitters and over time affects them adversely. When one is drinking alcohol, GABA is elevated momentarily, as opposed to glutamate, which increases steadily over time. Every time a person drinks alcohol, their GABA levels raise and then drop after the 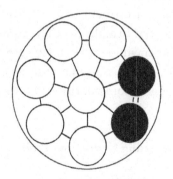 drug wears off, but a heavy drinker's glutamate remains elevated. Recall that glutamate is the agitating neurochemical of the brain. The residual elevated glutamate drives the person to drink more so that GABA (the calming neurochemical) will also increase.

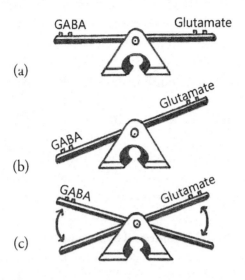

(a) The average person has plenty of GABA to counteract the agitation of their glutamate

(b) Once an alcoholic stops drinking, the imbalance between their high glutamate and low GABA can reach dangerous levels and even result in a grand mal seizure.

(c) The balance between the GABA and glutamate of an alcoholic changes with every drink the alcoholic takes. Alcoholics drink to raise their GABA to a level that will successfully counteract their glutamate.

When an active alcoholic suddenly stops drinking, they experience severe withdrawal. The GABA drops dramatically, creating a marked imbalance between GABA and glutamate. Glutamate, like race cars in the brain going hundreds of miles an hour with no stop signs, goes higher and higher, causing more and more agitation. This increases the severity of withdrawal symptoms and leads to delirium tremens. By the second or third day of quitting, the alcoholic starts to experience confusion, agitation, and the shakes. The periphery of the body is a strong indicator of what is happening internally. Tremulousness, shakes, sweaty palms, and hyper-agitation of the body are all symptoms of the elevated glutamate's effect in the brain. Soon enough, with such marked agitation of the brain and the glutamate being unopposed by the GABA system, a grand mal seizure can occur.

Physicians, nurses, and other health care professionals have noted that patients are severely agitated over the first 72 hours because of the high levels of glutamate. At the 72-hour mark, the glutamate suddenly stops rising and begins to decrease over time while the GABA levels slowly increase.

Levels of Acute Alcohol Withdrawal Syndrome

Detoxification treatment is all about getting the patient's neurotransmitters back to their normal genetic state as safely as possible. The severity of withdrawal symptoms during detoxification depends *not* on the amount of alcohol they drank, but rather on the imbalance of their glutamate and GABA levels. Naturally, there are other factors involved such as malnutrition, mixed encephalopathy, and dehydration. Basically any factors that are related to the patient's imbalance of neurotransmitters determine the severity and progression of each individual's detoxification.

Patients in the hospital suffering from acute alcohol withdrawal syndrome (AWS) are classified in one of three levels: mild withdrawal, moderate withdrawal, or severe withdrawal. Patients with mild withdrawal are very shaky, but do not get delirium tremens. They experience some tremor as well as hypertension, and they do well with minimal medications. Their GABA to glutamate differential is temperate. Patients experiencing moderate alcohol withdrawal have a greater discrepancy between their GABA and glutamate levels. This greater imbalance puts the patient in a state of hypervigilance with a rapid heart rate, supraventricular tachycardia, and significant agitation. The patients experiencing severe alcohol withdrawal have glutamate that is exceedingly high and GABA that is incredibly low. They experience delirium tremens and other complications like visual hallucinations and possibly seizure activity. Patients who go into delirium tremens have glutamate so high that no matter what they do, they cannot raise GABA enough to balance out the calming versus agitation imbalance. These patients do not react to the normal benzodiazepines or medications that we utilize to raise GABA at the GABA1a site. Other GABA drugs must be used.

Combating Seizure Activity

The brain, being the dynamic and miraculously functioning organ that it is, has electrical waves going through it that cause a fascinating function and spinning of impulses. This enables us to think and assess our environment and choose how to react to it.

Electroencephalographic specialists and neurologists who diagnose different types of seizures put multiple wires on a patient's head and analyze various parts of the brain, looking for specific activity that could be abnormal. They have found that in certain areas of the brain, the brain cannot suppress very strong electrical waves and impulses; it is this inability that can lead to a focus of activity. That focus can suddenly increase in size, encompassing the entire brain, rendering it completely incapable of functioning. It is at this point that one loses consciousness, falls to the floor convulsing, and remains there for several minutes until finally regaining consciousness. Sometimes the patient will continue to convulse, having jerking motions and losing control of the bladder. That is an extended seizure, which is much more life threatening.

When this kind of grand mal seizure occurs during an alcohol detoxification, the cause is typically too much glutamate and not enough GABA activation to oppose it. Glutamate and GABA are in a continual balance act, and alcohol changes this balance for the worst. At first while drinking the alcohol, the GABA increases, providing drinkers with that cool, calm, collected feeling, giving them the confidence to go out and have a good time with minimal agitation. But the next day, the GABA drops below its natural level, leaving the person feeling a bit shaky. When this is repeated with enough frequency and high dosage, the glutamate will steadily rise. The drinker is creating a self-induced neurochemical imbalance, ultimately causing the craving for more alcohol.

The brain has an incredible ability to recall its past encounters with heavy drinking. Heavy drinking creates a neurochemical imbalance, altering the balance between GABA and glutamate (the neurotransmitter system responsible for seizure activity). If the alcoholic patient successfully detoxifies and gets off alcohol for several months, his or her glutamate slowly returns to its baseline. However, regardless of whether the patient remains sober or not, the brain never forgets the disproportionately high glutamate in relation to the low GABA. Years may pass without any alcohol consumption, but all it takes is one week of heavy drinking for an ex-alcoholic's glutamate to suddenly surge exceedingly high. This is the new natural response to the alcohol because the brain never forgets the level that it once had previously attained. It seeks that high level rapidly again when one drinks, making the person very anxious. The intensified cravings that follow are the body's way of trying to raise the GABA. Since the glutamate does not rise gradually like it used to, but rather returns to the highest level once reached, alcoholics who have ever experienced an alcohol-related seizure will face that threat for the rest of their lives. The threat of grand mal seizure activity will remain forever, regardless of the duration of their sobriety.

Individuals at risk of the reoccurrence of grand mal seizures absolutely need an *inpatient* detoxification. Recall that GABA acts as the stop signs throughout the brain for the glutamate, which when unchecked by GABA, are like out-of-control racecars revving up the brain. It is when the glutamate reaches such a height that it passes through an ionosphere-like suppression, and the GABA can no longer curb the hyperactivity of the brain. It is at this point that convulsions commence and grand mal seizures occur. Patients in that situation have responded well to GABA drugs like Ativan, Valium, Tegretol, Neurontin, or antiseizure drugs in order to temporarily increase the GABA to a high enough level that prevents the glutamate from causing a grand mal seizure.

How to Use the GABA System during the Detoxification Phase of Treatment

I frequently utilize the GABA system when treating alcoholics for both their initial detoxification and for suppressing their cravings. When doing so, there are some key things to remember. Alcohol activates the GABA system, which is closely tied to the opiate system. Due to this close association, we can use the GABA system's receptor sites to treat both alcohol and opiate-related detoxification problems. Though the GABA receptor sites have proven quite useful, I refrain from using the GABA1a site (which is activated by benzodiazepines such as Valium) any more than just a few days because of the unpredictability of the site. This unpredictability is a direct result of physicians frequently abusing it.

Most physicians and intensive care specialists know to use the GABA system when treating AWS but unfortunately limit themselves to using only the GABA1a site, with a Valium product usually being the drug of choice. This method typically proves unsuccessful, and the brain continues going so fast (due to the high glutamate) that it cannot retrieve information from the temporal lobe, nor can it sense visually or aurally what is occurring in its surroundings. The patient then experiences delirium tremens and goes into a pre-seizure state. On top of that, too much benzodiazepine can change the billions of receptor sites throughout the brain that slow all circuits down. That is why the more the amount of Valium is increased, the more the patient experiences a sensation of fading out, until they fall asleep. They can get a similar effect with the use of phenobarbital, which is also a GABA drug, but works on different receptor sites throughout the brain.

During the detoxification process, when the patient is down-regulated with high glutamate, medications to raise GABA as high as possible and inhibit glutamate (like Neurontin and Lyrica) are used to stabilize the person. Antiseizure medications along with GABA drugs such as baclofen, Depakote, Lamictal, Tegretol, Dilantin, phenobarbital, and Robaxin have all been effective at sufficiently raising GABA, thereby decreasing the shakes, chronic tremulousness, and anxiety associated with unopposed glutamate. These drugs are chosen over others because they raise the level of GABA without activating the erratic GABA1a sites.

After facilitating numerous treatments for both detoxifications and anxiety disorders, positive results have been obtained by using phenobarbital for no more than seven or eight days. It cannot be stressed enough that there is absolutely no reason for a doctor to treat a patient by prescribing phenobarbital for longer than a few days. All levels of phenobarbital should be nontoxic. If someone is prescribed more than 500 milligrams of it in 24 hours, a blood test should be done to insure that the phenobarbital has not reached toxic levels. Not abiding by this rule can have disastrous effects of toxicity such as pulmonary complications, physical unsteadiness leading to falls, and extended stays in the general hospital or the ICU. I once had a patient who was driving her children around while having double the toxic levels of phenobarbital. This could have had terrible results. By using phenobarbital in a limited fashion, there have been excellent results in 8,000 inpatient detoxifications.

Medications to Suppress Cravings

Once the patient has gotten through the detoxification, we must then confront the issue of cravings. It is difficult to know immediately which neurotransmitters are low in each genetic alcoholic. We do know however, which neurotransmitters alcohol raises, providing a good starting point for indicating what imbalances possibly exist. Glutamate, as you recall is very toxic at high levels and greatly contributes to patients' craving for alcohol, and therefore needs to be countered out with a higher balance of GABA. GABA can be raised or balanced out with a drug called Campral. Campral is also a glutamate readjustment drug that can be utilized to battle craving. The Drug Index lists other GABA or GABA-like drugs such as Topamax, Neurontin, and other non-addictive drugs that have proven to be very effective. Many alcoholics also have serotonin deficiencies. In these cases, the patient's serotonin can be raised with a number of serotonin agonists, such as Lexapro, Paxil, or Prozac to name a few.

Blackout drinkers' treatment is often centered on the opiate and dopamine systems because they seek the euphoric high associated with the dopamine and opiate surge in the nucleus accumbens. Recent studies have shown that these blackout alcoholics do not even have to start drinking for this dopamine release to occur. Just looking at a glass of wine, or whatever alcoholic beverage they prefer, is enough to get their nucleus accumbens going, thus enhancing their desire to pick up that drink. Much like Pavlov's dogs salivating with the ring of a bell, the brains of these blackout drinkers react prior to actually drinking, and once the beverage is consumed, the dopamine release accelerates.

Competitive inhibitors like naltrexone appear to block that initial release of dopamine, thereby curtailing the alcoholic's cravings. Naltrexone or Vivitrol therefore can be used to block the dopamine and opiate system in the nucleus accumbens to suppress craving. It typically inhibits the euphoric opiate effect of alcohol that leads to blackout drinking. The drugs mentioned in this section are just a part of the arsenal that can be used to target the cravings of each alcoholic, with their unique heredity genome.

Alcohol has an agonistic effect on the endocannabinoid system, but as an addictionologist I do not believe in using cannabis to treat alcohol cravings. Though cannabis activates CB1 or CB2 receptor sites, the use of narcotics to treat alcoholics is not a viable option. It is true that using cannabis will activate their opiate center, thereby decreasing their cravings for alcohol, however in a short while there will be a new addiction to treat. Trading one addiction for another just leads to more misery for the patient and is not a practical solution.

In some severe cases where the alcoholic has endured major consequences, we start off trying to hit every neurotransmitter we can. Once they have attained sobriety, we back off on some of the neurotransmitter modulators. Unfortunately after months of sobriety, some people relapse on alcohol within three or four days of running out of their medications. Some drugs work profoundly well on most patients, and not very well on others, demonstrating that we cannot always successfully assess the patient's balance of neurotransmitters in the initial evaluation. To meet the physical needs of patients, it usually takes some time to fully understand which neurotransmitter imbalance we are up against and how each individual is "wired."

Brain Rules

Rule #32: When detoxifying patients with severe alcohol withdrawal syndrome, one is actually treating the imbalance of GABA versus glutamate.

Rule #33: How severe the withdrawal symptoms are depends directly on the extent of the GABA and glutamate imbalance and needs to be modulated with appropriate medications at different GABA sites.

Rule #34: Once a grand mal alcohol withdrawal seizure has occurred, there is a 70 percent chance of another grand mal seizure occurring in the future if one starts to drink heavily again.

Rule #35: An alcoholic's body becomes conditioned after years of intermittent drinking and sobriety, thus if he or she begins to consume alcohol in large quantities ever again, within a few days the body down-regulates and the rapidly increased level of glutamate becomes highly toxic.

"Drugs and alcohol can act like a mucky filter for our perceptions, distorting the way the brain imprints memories…"

Chapter 9

Memory and
Chemical Dependency

It was a typical Monday morning for Sharon Campbell, or so it seemed.[11] She puts on her make-up and thinks to herself, "Last night was a rough one, but at least I slept the whole night through." She feels a bit groggy, but reasons, "Who doesn't on a Monday morning?" With her business suit on and all ready to go, she grabs her purse and hurries into the kitchen.

"What are you doing here?" she exclaims. "Aren't you going to be late for work!?!"

Her husband just glairs back at her as he sips his coffee and nods his head, signaling her to open the door leading to the garage. She opens the door to find a mangled wreck of a car. Horrified, she demands to know how this happened.

"You did the same thing to *my* car last week. Now neither of us have any way of getting to work," he replies disgusted and matter-of-factly.

---

11 Names in this book have been changed.

"Blackout again," is the only explanation she can think of, but she still cannot believe her eyes. She looks at the car and looks back at her husband, wondering how she could have caused this mess and yet not remember a thing. All she honestly remembers from the night before is that she slept well.

Imprinting Memories

Sadly, this is based on a true story. Sharon later checked the local newspaper to see if the police were looking for a red sports car that had caused major damages or worse yet, to make sure no one had been killed in a hit-and-run accident the night before. She found nothing, but checked the front of her car just in case to make sure there was no blood. None was visible. She wondered how her body could be completely intact, while her car had been absolutely totaled.

On the kitchen counter were the medications for sleep she had taken the night before. She had had a few drinks with them and must have completely blacked out. *Blacking out* should not be confused with *passing out*. When someone blacks out, they continue to function, but neurochemically cannot imprint a complete memory in their temporal lobe of recent or current events. As noted here, the consequences can be devastating. Chemical dependency's effect on an individual's memory system can result in drastic physical effects and strained relationships. Drugs and alcohol can act like a mucky filter for our perceptions, distorting the way the brain imprints memories, but some of those consequences can be largely reversed through detoxification programs such as AA.

Memory – How it Works and How it is Altered

We rely on memory to execute even the simplest of tasks throughout our day-to-day lives. Both short-term and long-term memories play a crucial role in determining how we understand our surroundings and experience life. Most of our memories are tied to images. For instance, if someone were to ask you the address of the house you grew up in, accompanying your reply, an image would likely be brought to mind. We carry a tremendous amount of these kinds of images in the part of the brain called the *temporal lobe*, which acts like our memory disk. It is here where we store both hard data, like the exact location and address of your house, and the images associated with that information.

Our human CPU, the mid forebrain bundle, is responsible for creating memories and calling them back to mind. It processes our

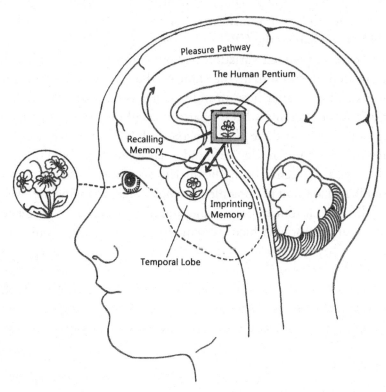

Millions of times a minute, information gets sent through the mid forebrain bundle (our CPU), as we receive and retrieve data. The pleasure pathway, with all its neurotransmitters, regulates that CPU, which processes all information. By altering neurotransmitter levels, drugs and alcohol can act like a mucky filter for our perception, distorting the way the brain imprints memories.

environment and retrieves information, both placing the images and data on the temporal lobe, and recalling them. This ability is taken for granted, because millions of times a minute, we are sending information through our CPU, receiving and retrieving data. When we see something in front of us, we look at it, visualize it, image it, and then use past and present information to tell us what that image is and how we are going to negotiate through life with those images.

The biggest difference between the brain's CPU and a computer's CPU is *feelings*, which are controlled by human things like hormones and neurotransmitters. Contrary to the brain, which is subject to change, the CPU in a computer is hard-wired; it does not have very much variation in how it processes the data and programming put into it. The brain, on the other hand, is dynamic in its ability to alter how an individual sees an image. There is a nucleus, or "steering wheel," that comes off of the mid forebrain bundle and is called the *pleasure pathway*. It is here that many of the neurotransmitters' nuclei are found, such as the locus coeruleus and the ventral tegmental area. The nucleus accumbens also contains a significant amount of dopamine and opiates. By changing the levels of these neurotransmitters, drugs and alcohol have the power to alter our memories (which is essentially just data stored within our brain). They do so by affecting the pleasure pathway, which regulates the CPU. Therefore, when a person under the influence of drugs or alcohol perceives a real image or actual occurrence from their environment, as the data goes through the CPU, it gets filtered or changed in an awkward way as it is placed in the temporal lobe.

Flashbacks and Blackouts

The effects of either drinking alcohol or using opiates to the point of blacking out are often devastating on many levels. When drinkers' blood alcohol levels reach between .24 to .30, the brain's ability to encode memories is hampered and memory becomes fragmented. Blood alcohol levels are going up and down like a wave.

Things that occur on the lower part of the wave are remembered, while the things that happen on the upper part, when the BAC peaks, are never recorded. That is fragmented memory.

Blackouts not only impair the mind's ability to imprint accurate memories onto individuals' temporal lobes, they also can lead to flashbacks. During a blackout or the near-blackout state, up to half of the information in an individual's surroundings that a non-intoxicated person would naturally commit to memory, can be lost. People who claim they cannot remember what happened the night before because they blacked out, quite literally *cannot* remember because the information that might normally be imprinted was not imprinted onto the temporal lobe. Intoxication to the point of blackout leaves the memories of individuals to literally bits and pieces, because that is all that was ever imprinted – bits and pieces.

Blackout drinkers and blackout opiate users (people who regularly use these substances to the point of blacking out) sometimes suffer from episodes of inexplicable fear, which some refer to as *flashbacks*. This often happens when these patients first come off drugs and alcohol. The individual will all of the sudden become very fearful and afraid, not even aware themselves of what in their environment ignited this fear. Often times something in the environment will spark the previous alcohol- or drug-abusers' memory of something bad that happened while they were intoxicated. But since blackouts leave individuals with only partial images or memories, when that incomplete data comes back to mind, they are unable to make the association and identify what it is causing the fear. So the only thing placed in the temporal lobe during the blackout was something frightful, but the person is unable to know what is causing the fear they are currently experiencing.

The best way to help individuals get through these flashbacks is to help them understand that they have no immediate threat. They first have to be made conscious of the fact that they are afraid. They must try to analyze the environment around them to find out what is causing them to suddenly become very afraid or have a panic attack. If they can do this, they can then try to understand both why they are frightened and emotional at that point in time, and that whatever it is that triggered the flashback is no longer going to be a future threat. It takes a lot of work to do this.[12]

Altered Data Means Inaccurate Memories

We need accurate memories or valid data in order to function properly. We use data from computers all the time, and we naturally assume that data is correct. Computers need valid data so they can process old and new information correctly. We rely on the data (the information stored as memories) within our brain and consider it to be valid, but when under the influence of drugs or alcohol, these substances filter our external awareness and senses, often times rendering the data placed into the temporal lobes as bad or incorrect. With incorrect data, one cannot be certain as to what is truth and what is not.

Cocaine and methamphetamine are infamous for their effect on the brain's CPU. When people use these drugs, there is a lot of dopamine involved within the locus coeruleus, which modulates the CPU in a certain way, making images become very weird. People on high-dose cocaine or methamphetamine become very bizarre and paranoid; often they fear narcotics officers are outside the window ready to get them. They are suspicious and unsure of their surroundings. At this point, not only are they delving into a false reality around them, they are also putting some information into their data banks that will be used later in a very awkward way because of its inaccuracy.

Intuition

Our initial reaction to people and things is our intuition at work – the feeling we get, devoid of any explanation or use of our

---

12 I highly recommend *Ten Ways to Reduce Stress*, written by Claire Wheeler M.D., Ph.D. for more information on analyzing and re-imaging data.

reasoning process. Our intuition is developed through past experiences. For example, a lot of the over-all emotions people experience when reacting to being around their family come from intuition. Intuitiveness or intuition is a perception of something that comes to us within the blink of an eye. It is automatic. We have a feeling, but we do not know nor can we explain why we have it. Another example of intuition is when someone taps you on the shoulder and says, "Hi, remember me?" For the life of you, you cannot place the face, but immediately you are overcome with either a good feeling or a "get away from me" feeling. No other information or data about this person emerges in your mind; all you have is a feeling. *That* is intuition.

Intuitive feelings are based on data in the temporal lobe that does not resurface in the form of images. Incidentally, the data that individuals draw their intuitive feelings from can be inaccurate. That data could have been placed in the temporal lobe from abnormal feelings altered by drugs or alcohol. Over time, drug and alcohol users store distorted data repeatedly. This distortion can cause their feelings towards the people around them – be it a spouse, a child, or a boss, to become very bizarre and of little value due to the unreliability of their data. How individuals with chemical dependency problems view the people around them can become drastically distorted. The incomplete and deceiving data processed and placed into their temporal lobes as memories, has the power to severely damage or destroy relationships.

Fixing Perceptions and Reframing Data

An important part of coming off of drugs or alcohol is correcting the data in the temporal lobe. Drugs and alcohol can distort your intuition so severely, that it can alter your feelings toward your own family. The only way to fix these distorted feelings (which come from images and data placed in the chemically dependent individuals' temporal lobe) toward intimate associates is to gather *new* data while sober. Chemically dependent patients need to gather and put in new data while they are sober so that these images leading to uneasy intuitive feelings can be reframed.

When detoxifying patients in the chemical dependency unit, we take them off of the drugs that are causing the distortion of images and senses so that they can start gathering new data that have substantiated validity. Once they have been successfully detoxified and the detoxification medications wear off, we try to keep them in the chemical dependency unit for three or four weeks, where they will not be further exposed to drugs. Meanwhile, patients' own neurotransmitters are balancing out and returning to their natural levels so that they can now gather accurate information from their surroundings and process it in a clear and correct way. This enables them to take the old, bizarre, and distorted images and data stored in their temporal lobes as memories, and reframe them over the course of the three or four weeks.

Twenty-eight-day programs provide the perfect amount of time for neurochemicals to return to their natural balance, for cleaning out and reframing the data within the temporal lobe, and for substantiating what is happening in patients' lives. AA is founded on a twelve-step program, eight of which go into the complications and problems that people have had over the course of their alcohol use, demonstrating the importance of cleaning out old data and replacing it with new data. These steps start out with individuals acknowledging that they have a problem that has taken over their lives, basically admitting that their data banks are completely disheveled. By step four, individuals understand that they must make an assessment of their data bank, doing a fearless moral inventory. By step eight, they are confronting others with the goal of making amends with any whom they have harmed. This is where they get the help of others to straighten out the data in their minds of what *really* happened. This is a pivotal point in the recovery process of any alcoholic or other chemically dependent patient. They ask individuals in their lives what really happened in the past while they were on drugs or drinking. They enter this corrected data in to their understanding, thereby finding accurate reasoning behind all the events that are happening in their lives. Doing so, they can reframe those old images of what occurred in the past and discern reasonably where the fault lies. This is my assessment and understanding of how the brain works and why the twelve steps were written.

Straightening out the data within one's mind can be likened to straightening out the data of a business. Let's say the system the data was stored in got a virus, and now all the data is distorted and bad. After realizing she has a problem, the owner now needs to call up every business and every individual she has an account with. She would start by calling up associates she thinks owe her money and compare her data with theirs. She would acquire receipts and other billing data so that the record would have validity. She would then call her bill collectors and try to settle every account until finally she had all the data straightened out, so she could utilize it, treating it as a sure thing. Like a business, that is how our brain works. Having clear and accurate data allows individuals to get on with their lives and solve problems. Correcting the information within their temporal lobes, allows patients to react with their family members, co-workers, and friends in a very confident manner, knowing that the data that they now have is valid. Though it only takes three or four weeks of being off drugs or alcohol for patients' neurotransmitters to return to their proper balance, it may take months or years thereafter to correct the distorted data. Regardless of the arduousness of this task, it is a very important step to recovery.

Brain Rules

Rule #36: Drugs and alcohol influence neurotransmitters in a way that causes individuals' perception to be altered, thus distorting the way the brain imprints memories. For example, while a person blacks out, they continue to function, but neurochemically cannot imprint a complete memory in the temporal lobe.

Rule #37: The mid forebrain bundle, our brain's CPU, processes the environment around us, placing the images and data in the temporal lobe in the form of memories. It both creates and retrieves memories. The pleasure pathway regulates the mid forebrain bundle. Drugs and alcohol alter the neurotransmitter levels, especially those heavily concentrated in the above-mentioned locations, thereby altering individuals' perception and memories.

Rule #38: Blackouts that result from heavy alcohol or opiate use impair the brain's ability to imprint accurate memories, leading to inaccurate intuitive feelings and skewed or all-together lost data.

Rule #39: We rely on our memories to make sense of the world around us, but when drugs or alcohol filter our external awareness, senses, and perception, rendering the memory data incorrect, an individual can no longer be certain as to what is truth and what is not.

Rule #40: The incomplete and deceiving data processed and stored as memories in chemically dependent people has the power to severely alter or destroy relationships by providing an inaccurate concept. The only way for the chemically dependent individual to fix this is to collect new data on those relationships while sober – reforming their intuition and understanding. This is an important part of any 28-day program.

"No matter how severe the chemical dependency case and its resulting health complications are, focusing on the patients' neurotransmitter systems when choosing which medications to administer bears optimal results."

Chapter 10

Assisting Alcoholics and Addicts: Through Negotiations and in the Intensive Care Unit

Alcoholism touches the lives of many in our society whether directly or indirectly. In the United States alone, 7 percent of the population has some sort of drug or alcohol problem. Other countries reflect a similar if not greater incidence. Alcoholism and other chemical dependency problems are the top admitting diagnoses into community hospitals. Often alcoholism and addiction are coupled with financial instability and familial discord. Additionally, alcoholics and addicts frequently suffer psychological consequences like depression and severe health problems that can result in hospitalization. Many times the final straw that incites a need for negotiations, detoxification, and recovery are legal consequences such as DUIs or arrests.

Alcoholism, like any drug addiction, often makes a person think and act unreasonably, leading to frustration for all those around them such as family, doctors, and other medical staff. To combat this unreasonableness and reach some sort of resolution, those negotiating with an alcoholic must have an educated approach toward leveraging the alcoholic into sobriety. Much is at stake in these situations – not only the life of the alcoholic, but also the well-being and happiness of all those around him or her. Sometimes the situation might call for a surprise intervention where catching the alcoholic off-guard for negotiations gives the family significant leverage.

Psychodynamics of an Alcoholic Resisting Treatment

To add to the difficulty of negotiations, many alcoholics and addicts also have underlying psychiatric problems such as major depressive episodes, bipolar manic depression, and/or attention deficit disorder. These kinds of patients tend to be irrational and hard to deal with. Since their cognitive and associative processes are skewed due to either alcoholism or drug addiction, it is difficult for them to grasp the gravity of the situation at hand. They often view the problem as extending beyond the issue of drugs or alcohol, and when confronted about the issue, see it as an attack on their own self-esteem and worth. The psychiatric problems definitely cloud the real item of negotiation – their alcohol consumption and their need for either complete abstinence or the curtailing of their habit.

Alcoholics and addicts lack a clear mind; they think and act differently. An individual trying to negotiate with an alcoholic or addict should do a thorough assessment of their mental condition before proceeding. Doctors must determine whether or not patients are intoxicated and/or depressed and in need of psychological treatment. There are a number of neurochemical abnormalities related to genetics that can contribute to patients' tendency towards denial and refusal to negotiate. Even after their actions have led to their hospitalization, they may still deny that their drug use or alcohol consumption is a problem. Alcoholics and addicts have other psycho-motivated incentives (such as cravings) that have a strong hold on their reasoning ability and cognition.

Alcoholics have a neurotransmitter-based modulated abnormality of thought in the mid forebrain bundle, causing them to have both an innate need for alcohol consumption and feelings of denial. Feelings of pressure, as well as an inclination to isolate themselves, renders many alcoholics and addicts incapable of working out their problems. The shame and loss of self-esteem they feel after being discovered can drive them to further measures of isolation. Often times they would rather leave their home and get a divorce than face the pressure of dealing with their disease. As long as they are drinking, they feel like they can handle these pressures. While sober, the pressure from the physician and their family feels overwhelming and they fear it will continue even if they were to stop drinking or using drugs.

Health Problems

Health problems are another avenue of trouble for alcoholics that can land them in the Intensive Care Unit (ICU). It is not uncommon for alcoholics to have significant medical problems and end up being hospitalized and even put on a ventilator. Seizures, hepatic withdrawal, and liver failure are just a few of the complications associated with alcoholism. Liver failure can cause additional problems such as high ammonia, which in turn causes confusion. In these situations, it is more than likely not a good time to initiate negotiations. However patients in the hospital may suddenly come to the realization (if they are cognizing correctly) that alcohol was the root cause of their hospitalization. They may even realize that the vomiting of blood, hepatic failure, heart disease, or seizure activity they have been experiencing likely resulted from the alcohol abuse.

Hospitalization can be a real eye-opener for some alcoholics.

When admitted to the hospital with complications from their al-coholism, alcoholics' confrontational stance might actually soften, with them now considering death as a possible outcome. Once detoxified, an alcoholic becomes much more reasonable and open to negotiations. An alcoholic who is drunk or intoxicated lacks the mental faculties, judgment, insight, and cognition necessary to understand the consequences of their actions, and why they need to quit. The reality of the hospital setting, as well as the alcoholic's obvious illness and how it is related to the alcohol are helpful fac-tors in giving the physician and family leverage for negotiations.

Methods of Negotiation:
Dealing with Alcoholics and Addicts Successfully

There are a lot of lies and deceit that are often disclosed during detoxification and recovery. Part of the recovery process is repairing relationships. Sadly though, sometimes the damage is beyond repair even when the alcoholic or addict wants to recover. Regardless, one of the best negotiation tools is for the spouse and doctor to ensure the alcoholic that the relationship will continue.[13] However, the alcoholic should be aware that there will likely be distrust in future family affairs.

During a family crisis, the alcoholic or drug addict is not the only one lacking in listening abilities. Often the entire family is so emotional and filled with anger, no one listens to each other and therefore nothing gets accomplished. The rule of listening 80 percent and talking 20 percent is not the typical scenario for these kinds of negotiations. Often times the family's anger is tied up with various fears and misunderstandings about the alcoholic, which all contribute to hindered communication. While the spouse is often filled with inward and outward expressions of anger, there is usually very little verbal communication on the part of the alcoholic. Typi-cally when faced with confrontation about their habit, the alcoholic

---

13 Almost all references to alcoholics in this section, also can apply to persons addicted to other various drugs.

or addict will be very quiet and passive, adding to the difficulty of negotiating. On the other hand, they might become very angry, walking out and yelling. All these emotions from both sides disrupt the ability to successfully negotiate the need for recovery.

The best approach for initiating negotiations with the alcoholic in the family is to remain calm and try to be understanding. Equipping oneself with educated concepts of alcoholism and addiction and negotiation methods learned through some sort of counseling, such as Al-Anon, gives an individual the tools necessary for more successful negotiations. Having a supportive approach with the alcoholic often works much better than an abrasive methodology. If this doesn't work, perhaps a professional interventionist or a professional negotiator with experience in this area can be hired. Of course they must be informed about all the issues and consequences of the addiction and given all the needed data about the alcoholic.

Often interventions are performed by surprise. The most effective interventions are conducted with much care, understanding, and the presentation of facts. Ideally when the alcoholic walks into the intervention, he or she is not under the influence of any drugs or alcohol and is in a reasonable mood. The concerned family members express their love, understanding, and reasons for wanting the alcoholic to be sober. Expressing the need for change with the utmost respect for the alcoholic, the interventionist acts to negotiate some type of a recovery plan.

During the negotiations, alcoholics feel they cannot deal with the family and that they need the calming effect that they get from the alcohol or drugs in the future. They feel that there is nothing to gain from going to the hospital to detoxify. Many alcoholics reason that their spouses married them knowing they were alcoholics, therefore they should just find a way to deal with the alcoholism. This combative attitude is internally countered by the addict's understanding of their family's needs and their expression of love.

Many spouses of alcoholics have found the hardball ultimatum to work well. Laying down the law causes the alcoholic to seek recovery once they know that if they don't change their ways, they will have to leave their home and face being homeless. That kind of ultimatum, when given at short notice and in a matter-of-fact way, allows the alcoholic to escape into a recovery program. The alcoholic often sees this recovery program as an opportunity to mull over a plan of future negotiations with their spouse; in a sense they are buying time. Though difficult to perform, this hardball type of ultimatum from a spouse is a very effective negotiation tool for both sides. It gives the alcoholic or addict the ability for to walk out and have at least some dignity while making up their own mind to go into an alcohol or drug unit. For this to work, the alcoholic must know that he or she has a home and relationship to return to if he or she recovers.

Family love, as well as hope for a future life together, both serve as positive leverage for the family. It is important that the addict or alcoholic individual understands that all present in the negotiations are there out of concern for him or her. Love and understanding are the best negotiation tools a family can have. Many family members can ease conflict by initially and continually disclosing their love for the alcoholic, but they must be prepared for a long and difficult negotiation.

A Look at the ICU

The ICU is filled with the severest cases of drug abuse and tolerance. These are the patients who, in addition to issues of withdrawal, have multiple medical, surgical, and possibly even psychiatric problems. The resulting anxiety and confusion leaves them in an unreasonable state of mind. Every day, ICU doctors and nurses tend to these patients who do not cooperate with medical care. When they wake up, they often become so anxious and disillusioned that they attempt to pull out their endotracheal tubes or IVs. As a result, many patients end up being on ventilators for extended periods of time. The complications that ensue and costs that accrue from these cases of extended reliance on a ventilator are innumerable, and these patients often end up suffering from pneumonia and other pulmonary diseases. They also decompensate rapidly because of their compromised nutritional state and multiple other factors too copious to list here. These extended stays on ventilators and the consequential medical complications result in millions, if not billions, of dollars in extra hospitalization and treatment costs. If ICU medical staff were to embrace the methods of care that I employ every day, not only would it be far more cost effective, but more importantly, patients would be cared for in a quicker, safer, and more efficient way.

Some of the most challenging cases I have assisted with involve heavy drinkers who go into the hospital for a surgery and then suddenly go into acute withdrawal and end up in the ICU on a ventilator. The eight neurotransmitter systems are extremely important to utilize when a patient is going through withdrawal and is in acute detoxification. I cannot emphasize enough how imperative it is to understand what these systems are doing in the withdrawal state and how predictable they act in each phase of detoxification. That knowledge is usually lacking among hospital based physicians who have to treat chemical dependency in the ward or in the ICU. That lack of knowledge or training needs to be remedied because up to 50 percent of county hospital admissions have some sort of chemical dependency problem. I have done hundreds of ICU detoxifications with people on or off ventilators and that knowledge consistently rewards me with the improvement of the patients' care within 72 hours of adjusting medications.

It is vital to know how each medication affects patients' neurotransmitter systems. Knowledge of these effects is a determining factor in deciding which medications to administer. Take for example modafinil. Modafinil is useful in cases where patients are hypersomnolent after over-dosing on dopamine stimulants such as methamphetamine or cocaine. It increases the stimulating effects of glutamate and noradrenaline and decreases the GABA, thus making these patients much more aware and alert. Within a half hour the patient is completely awake and, with the help of the nursing staff, is able to get off the ventilator, hence decreasing their length of stay in the ICU. During the administration of this drug, there is no increase in the patients' heart rate or blood pressure, which is highly advantageous for intensive care unit treatment. However, as with any other drug that increases the release of dopamine in the nucleus accumbens, modafinil must be used with caution since it could be addictive. Modafinil is only one of many drugs utilized in these kinds of complex cases. Multiple medications are administered that effect GABA production, the GABA-glutamate balance, serotonin agonistic and inhibitive qualities, noradrenergic modulation, and dopamine agonistic or antagonistic effects. The medical staff caring for these kinds of patients needs to understand their patients' conditions at a deeper level – the neurotransmitter level. That understanding will enable them to administer the safest and quickest treatment possible with an optimal outcome that in the end saves everyone – hospitals, insurance companies, and patients – a whole lot of money.

Strategies in the ICU

The method of focusing on a patient's balance of neurotransmitter systems throughout treatment works in even the most extreme cases. I am typically called into the ICU when the staff is faced with cardiac bypass patients or trauma patients who have been on multiple medications and the ventilator for over a week. When I get called into the ICU for these extreme detoxification cases, it is always my goal to get patients off ventilators and have them awaken within a 72 hour period. While I do not have the complete answer to all problems in the ICU, I do have 30 years of experience in hospital ICUs across the San Francisco East Bay, where time and time again I have successfully reached this goal. I have done so by adjusting the patients' balance of neurotransmitters.

When dealing with the eight neurochemical systems of the brain, there are certain principles that we follow with every one of our patients. The first step is to analyze the state of their eight systems by looking at their current situation and the medical problems that patient is up against. I conduct this analysis by talking to the family about any alcoholism, anxiety disorder, or post-traumatic stress disorder that this patient might have. I try to find out (1) if the patient is in detoxification from some drug, (2) if they are in withdrawal, (3) the amount of time since their last drink or use of drugs, and (4) if they have some sort of underlying psychiatric problems that will cause them to become very anxious when an attempt to remove their ventilator is made. Knowledge of each of these factors is vital to attaining successful results.

Many times we will find it has been over a week since their last drink or encounter with drugs. Therefore, the medical staff might have placed them on Ativan (a benzodiazepine with a fifteen-hour half-life), Versed (another GABA drug with a shorter half-life), and/or high-dose narcotics. Many are on continuous drips of these drugs, leaving us unaware of the exact concentration in their system. Often these patients have had pneumonia or congestive heart failure, but their oxygenation and pulmonary status are hopefully improving at this point. Analyzing the current situation of the patient will usually provide me with enough information to successfully maneuver their treatment with two objectives in mind. The first objective is to have the patient wake up without anxiety or withdrawal so they will cooperate with the medical staff. This allows the second goal to be reached of having the patient extubated with good pulmonary function. Reaching these goals is quite a feat and takes a great deal of careful analysis.

While every patient's case is unique in the ICU, there are some basic generalities that we can extract and learn from. As I said from the onset, the human brain functions in a predictable manner. It is by paying attention to the patterns associated with its eight basic neurotransmitter systems and their reactions to detoxifications and various medications, that the medical staff in ICUs can offer the best treatment possible. No matter how severe the chemical dependency case and its resulting health complications are, focusing on the patients' neurotransmitter systems when choosing which medications to administer bears optimal results.

Brain Rules

Rule #41: An educated approach must be taken towards leveraging a person into sobriety. Love and understanding are the best negotiation tools a family can use to counter the addict's tendency towards denial, avoidance, and isolation.

Rule #42: Modafinil and Zonegran are two of many medications that are useful in the ICU for patients who have over-dosed on methamphetamine or cocaine because they raise glutamate and dopamine, waking the patient in a safe manner, making them alert, aware, and cooperative, with minimal agitation and no increase in heart rate or blood pressure. Many other medications are also excellent neurotransmitter tools. See our index.

Rule #43: Even in the most extreme cases of detoxification, patients in the ICU can be taken off the ventilator and awakened within 72 hours of adjusting their medications if their neurotransmitters are adjusted correctly. The pulmonary and cardiovascular statuses have to be stable.

Rule #44: Often what a detoxifying patient in the ICU needs in order to awaken and come off a ventilator with minimal anxiety is to be removed from all opiates and benzodiazepines, and instead given more predictable GABA and GABA-like drugs along with sedating propofol for their comfort.

Rule #45: Phenobarbital, Zonegran, modafinil and Precedex are useful medications in ICU, but they must be administered with caution. Always take into consideration neurochemical balances and their individual effects.

"I have made the statement hundreds of times, and I stand by it –
'Opiates can *cause* pain.'"

Chapter 11

Victims of the Opiate Craze

The other day I met Betty. Nine years on the very powerful narcotic called *fentanyl* had made her a prisoner to memory loss, isolation, and fear of life itself. Her family has been supporting her since she graduated from college, when one night she fell down some stairs. She never had any fractures nor did she ever go to the hospital. She just had pain. One thing led to the other and she ended up going from Vicodin to stronger and stronger drugs. One nasty spill down the stairs years ago, and now the main complaint was chronic nausea and abdominal pain, for which she took fentanyl. It took her nine years to realize that maybe the narcotics were what was *causing* the nausea and abdominal pain.

After some investigating, I found that both of her parents were alcoholics in recovery. "Bingo," I thought. Obviously there are some inherit deficiencies in her serotonin, or possibly GABA, glutamate, dopamine, or even noradrenaline systems. Betty actually never drank alcohol herself because the family had seen enough alcohol problems, but with alcoholism in the genes, this meant easily getting hooked on opiates. Why opiates? Because this overpowering, central-acting neurotransmitter system runs the show in raising the other systems. She has no craving for alcohol, yet she gets both an opiate effect and a dopamine effect from the fentanyl.

To make a long story short, the nausea and the vomiting were caused by the fentanyl. She tried other opiates and they did the same thing. We treated the cravings by looking into her family history which helped us to make an educated guess as to where neurochemically her deficiencies lie. This led us to give her a serotonin agent, a GABA-Glutamate modulator (see index for the options) and an opiate blocker after her detoxification (see index) to decrease any possible future cravings for alcohol once she got off the opiates.

During the first few days of going through opiate withdrawal, people experience an intensification of pain from any prior injuries. As a rule, if a patient has had injuries in the past, the withdrawal symptoms will go straight to those areas, making them swear that they need that opiate medication. However after five days without opiates, 90 percent of those patients who want off the drugs find the pain is either the same as when they were taking the opiates, of less intensity, or entirely gone. As for Betty, her nausea and abdominal pain were cured. I have made the statement hundreds of times, and I stand by it – "Opiates can *cause* pain."

In this day and age an alarming number of individuals, from high school students to professionals, are addicted to some type of opiate. In the San Francisco Bay Area alone, we are witnessing an epidemic of OxyContin, hydrocodone, morphine, and fentanyl abuse. In the detoxification unit, not a day goes by without treating one of these unfortunate victims of the opiate craze. It is affecting people of all ages for a wide spectrum of reasons. In this chapter we will focus on the three groups of people most readily affected: patients in need of pain management, genetic alcoholics, and bipolar individuals. We will also examine the reasons behind their addiction and some of the devastating effects of opiate abuse. While some opiate drugs do have their place in medical care, the detrimental repercussions of opiate use often far out-weigh the benefits.

Pain Management

Our own body produces the strongest opiate in the world – beta-endorphin, which is made by our proopiomelanocortin. Our body always produces the best key for locking into its receptor sites, thus this beta-endorphin is the most effective tool for stimulating our opiate system. As mentioned in chapter 5, using opiates suppresses our body's production of beta-endorphin, but after detoxification off opiates, that beta-endorphin will usually come back. Experts state that beta-endorphin production does not achieve its optimal level until approximately four to six weeks later, however in my experience it only takes ten to fifteen days. If our natural opiates are so strong, why do so many people suffering from pain management issues become addicted to externally produced opiate-derived drugs? The answer is multi-facetted.

Opiate drugs do indeed have their place in medical care. People with diseases like cancer or other complications that cause bona fide pain should have pain control. The problem occurs once they have healed and the patient then tries to stop using the drug. Morphine and codeine actually come from poppy plants, but pharmaceutical companies also produce synthetics. The pharmaceutical industry has only recently admitted to the addiction and withdrawal symptoms that can result from use of their physically and psychologically addictive drugs; it only took 30 or 40 years to do so.

When patients attempt to stop taking narcotics, they go into withdrawal and can no longer tell if the pain they feel is coming from their previous disorder or from the withdrawal. I believe that many patients intuitively recognize that they are addicted to the drug and keep taking it anyway, knowing that if they were to stop, they would have to experience withdrawal. Often they believe that their underlying pain has somewhat resolved or is tolerable without the use of high-dose narcotics, but keep taking them to avoid the pains of withdrawal. Others however, cannot differentiate between the pain of withdrawal and that of their original complications. When one stops taking the narcotic and begins going through withdrawal, intensification of pain will ensue at every site in the body previously injured, but once the detoxification is complete along with the cessation of withdrawal symptoms, the pain will either be less than or equal to the amount experienced while on the opiates or narcotics. When someone wants to get off the narcotics after multiple back surgeries or other causes of chronic pain syndrome, chances are their pain will be less than when they were actually taking the medication. At our chemical dependency detoxification facility, we have found that 90 percent of the time, our patients' pain is better, if not the same, after detoxifying off the narcotics. We have never turned away any chronic pain patients, and we use the best methods possible, not using any opiates to detoxify patients off of narcotics. The following chapter will cover in detail how we detoxify these chronic pain sufferers.

Cross-Addiction: Alcohol and the Opiate System

Opiates suppress cravings for alcohol. As a chemical dependency specialist, I have seen countless alcoholics exchange their alcohol for opiates. We call this *cross-addiction*, and it happens because the end result of heavy drinking and opiate abuse is the same: a euphoric dopamine surge. Many will quit their habit of drinking alcohol at high doses and start using opiates, usually becoming addicted to Vicodin, Norco, OxyContin, or even heroin. Socially, there are many possible reasons for this occurrence, namely because opiate addiction is much easier to hide. Who wants to smell like alcohol to raise their dopamine when they can use opiates instead?

Alcohol abuse has many negative signs and blatant symptoms, such as bad breath or slurred speech. Family members cognizant of the problem can easily discern if the drinking continues or not. If alcoholics try opiates, they soon find that similar effects can be obtained without the smell, and that is when the crossover from alcohol to opiate abuse usually occurs. Nevertheless, genetic alcoholics do not need to start out as active alcoholics to become cross-addicted. A phenomenon exists where a genetic alcoholic who has never touched alcohol in their entire life (usually because of having traumatic childhood experiences with abusive alcoholic parents) will get some dental or orthopedic procedure done, be introduced to opiates, and then rapidly become addicted.

Whatever the social reason behind these genetic alcoholics starting to abuse opiates, the neurochemical reason for being addicted to the narcotics is the same. For instance, both alcohol and opiates, when taken in high doses, induce a highly addictive dopamine surge. As you know, genetic alcoholics inherit deficiencies in one or more of the six neurotransmitter systems that alcohol momentarily raises. It just so happens that using opiates has a similar effect on those neurotransmitters to that of alcohol. The opiate neurotransmitter system has strong connections to all five of these other systems, especially the GABA system. The opiate system is the central and strongest out of all the neurotransmitters in the alcohol system; it dominates and affects all other neurotransmitter systems.[14] So essentially, using narcotics not only stimulates the opiate system, but also ends up stimulating the other five in the alcohol system. Genetic alcoholics who abuse opiates are using the opiate system to enhance the deficiencies of the other systems.

Bipolar Patients and the Opiate System

When determining the best treatment for individuals addicted to opiates, we always consider the balance of their neurotransmitter systems before taking action. We need to know what kind of underlying disorder we are up against. If the patient is not dealing with issues of pain control and there is no indication of them being a genetic alcoholic, we probe to see if beneath the veneer of an opiate addict there lies a bipolar disorder. Some opiate abusers are aware they have a bipolar disorder; however, just as some genetic alcoholics are unaware of their predisposition towards alcoholism

---

14 The term *alcohol system* refers to the six combined neurotransmitter systems that are affected by alcohol.

and addiction, there also exist opiate abusers unaware that they are using opiates to suppress an undiagnosed bipolar disorder. Our job as addictionologists is to uncover and bring to light these disorders so we can then administer the most effective treatments.

No one is absolutely certain as to what the cause of the bipolar disorder is, but we do know that they bounce between the south pole of severe depression and the north pole of extreme agitation. People without any mood disorder live their lives somewhere along the equator – a temperate zone. Often, while at the south pole of depression, they just lay in bed wanting to take some medication to get them out of the funk they are in. It is common for patients aware of their disorder to replace their regular bipolar GABA medications with opiates like OxyContin and morphine. This stimulation of the opiate system in turn affects the GABA system and alleviates some of the bipolar symptoms, but the use of these heavy opiates also bring about an entirely new set of problems. They now face addiction, sedation, and a feeling of loss of control. Many bipolar patients come into our detoxification unit, heavily involved with opiates, wanting off these drugs.

It appears that bipolar patients have a GABA or calming disorder. We know this because general treatment protocol for bipolar patients is to put them on GABA drugs such as Depakote, Trileptal, and others. Sometimes we also add a little dopamine to their drug regimen. Dopamine is supposedly somewhat inhibitory to the opiate system. I am not sure how that relationship exists, but I do know that if we give bipolar patients dopamine at low doses, they seem to calm down and are in better control. However, when giving dopamine, there is a very fine threshold between not enough and too much. With too much dopamine, patients become agitated and start hallucinating; with not enough, they are severely depressed.

I have been trying to get a clearer understanding of the dopamine system with bipolar patients, and it has been challenging. What I have learned is that whatever you do with this system, you have to do it slowly, especially when detoxifying bipolar patients off opiates, taking into account how the opiate system that it is inhibiting is involved. One way or another, one must always remember that the GABA system is there to help soothe the opiate system as we detoxify the patients. Recall that the GABA and opiate systems are closely tied, like a husband and wife. The opiate system (the husband) is very strong but cannot talk. On the contrary, the GABA system (the wife) has many receptor sites and is quite talkative while she is holding her husband's hand. What we do to the GABA system helps the opiate system to up-regulate more smoothly. We have used this method time and again in cases of bipolar patients.

Bipolar patients, whether they are aware of their mood disorder or not, can typically control their bipolar symptoms by using opiates. Taking away the opiates during detoxification will change a patient's personality and reveal whether the patient is bipolar or not. If after two or three days of detoxifying a patient off of the opiates, he or she becomes manic, out of control, talkative, and hypervigilant, the patient is bipolar. This may or may not have been diagnosed or recognized over the years that they were taking opiates. This is because the opiate use has allowed them to control their bipolar disorder, and now that the opiates are gone, the other neurotransmitter systems' imbalances, including GABA, have surfaced. It then becomes obvious that their addiction to opiates was driven by the neurochemical imbalances associated with an underlying bipolar disorder.

The Devastating Effects of Opiate Abuse

Opiates destroy an individual's ability to cope with reality. Life is a struggle, and every day we are faced with good and bad. To have experienced a euphoric state while on opiates makes facing reality unappealing and difficult, ruining people's ability to cope with life's issues. It is not easy feeling normal thereafter. As I mentioned in the genetics chapter, it took me twenty years to realize something very important about addicts – they are never satisfied with feeling "normal."

I recently gave a lecture to some 40 opiate addicts and told them that ever since they had been on opiates, they had no idea of what it feels like to be normal because opiates had altered their very concept of normal. They do not understand why, since they have been on opiates, they continuously want to feel better or at a higher level. The reason is they have been conditioned, and feeling "normal" is no longer a satisfactory state of being for them. Why is that? The explanation is simple if you recall the B57 (serotonin deficient) rat studies mentioned in chapter 4. These studies demonstrated that the rats will continue to drink in spite of already having improved serotonin levels. So essentially the patient (or the rat) has been conditioned repeatedly, each time they dose themselves, to feel better. No matter how well they feel, they want to feel better than they did hours before. Whereas feeling normal is a perfectly acceptable and ideal baseline for non-drug users, a feeling of euphoria is the new baseline for drug abusers. Even after they recover, they will refer back to their baseline as feeling euphoric. Over time some of that conditioned response fades, unless the brain gets strong cues that cause re-emergence of memories and methods to ameliorate their present emotional or physical pain.

Using opiates has a significant effect on hormones as well. For instance, taking enough opiates (e.g. four to five Vicodin a day) will suppress the brain's regulatory system and production of testosterone in men. Typically three to four weeks after taking patients off opiates, their testosterone levels return to normal. After 28 days of sobriety, not only are patients physically better, but their hormone systems are also better. Total recovery really starts happening three to four weeks later. But hormones are not the only things affected by narcotics.

Opiates' effects are incredibly far reaching; they alter the very fabric of users' reality, and modify their perception by over years of use gradually dulling the acuity of their five senses. Not only do opiates hinder people's ability to see colors, they also alter memories. Many people on opiates are highly cognizant of its effects. Often patients come to me expressing that they need to take care of their children or grandchildren, but they feel the opiates they are on are robbing them of fully experiencing their life. They feel like they are missing out on something that the narcotics take away from them. A recent Canadian study indicated that people who are on addictive doses of opiates have a 300 percent accident rate. We have had patients who have detoxified off opiates that go outside to take a walk in the garden and come back in astonished at the beauty in the surroundings, beauty that they had been missing out on, in part because their perception of color was dulled. They also see smiles and expressions on children's faces that they say they have never noticed before.

We had one patient with rods in her back that had gone through multiple back surgeries and needed to be detoxified off opiates. When the treatment was complete and she went back home to her husband, she felt like she hardly knew him. This was because she had been living her life in a state of half blackout. It was very frightening to be with him since it was like an entirely new experience for her, not knowing who her husband was. After living with him for five years, this was the first time she had ever felt that way. Opiates impede people's ability to be fully aware of their surroundings, which is why it is essential to get people off of these narcotics.

Clearly, opiates are physically *and* mentally addictive. Perhaps the worst result of opiate abuse is what was discussed in chapter 5 of this book – the reality that extended opiate use causes modification of the opiate receptors that will last a lifetime. Once tolerance to the opiate system is built, the individual will never lose that tolerance. The pharmaceutical industry, though they finally admitted that their opiate drugs are addictive, never discusses the fact that people who abuse these opiates, will pay with zero pain tolerance later in life. What the pharmaceutical company produces and allows to happen is both unethical and immoral because of the danger intrinsic to what happens to the brain's receptor sites over time. In spite of all this danger, treatment to get people off opiates is improving, as you will see in the next chapter.

Brain Rules

Rule #46: The opiate system is the most dominant out of all the neurotransmitter systems, acting as the central axis of the other seven systems.

Rule #47: Ninety percent of patients taking narcotics for pain management experience less or the same amount of pain once their detoxification is complete, with the elimination of opiate addiction's side effects.

Rule #48: Cross addiction between alcohol and opiates is common because both opiates and alcohol affect the same set of neurotransmitters in a similar fashion.

Rule #49: Many people who abuse opiates are self-medicating their bipolar disorder, leading to other problems like addiction. Undiagnosed bipolar patients with their symptoms hidden by opiates, have their mood disorder become apparent once detoxification occurs.

Rule #50: Among the serious side effects of abusing opiates, are its dulling of the five senses and its distortion of reality.

Rule #51: Continued opiate use causes modification of the opiate receptor sites that will last a lifetime.

"Always remember that all of the neurotransmitter systems are connected and talk to one another and most alcoholics and drug addicts are born with deficiencies in their neurotransmitter levels. As addictionologists, we must get to the heart of our patients' cravings."

Chapter 12

Treating Opiate Addiction

Steven is a 24-year-old opiate-dependent patient who comes from a family of alcoholics. He has recently been detoxified off OxyContin and when returning to the detoxification unit, he states that he is craving opiates again. Thanks to the help of the serotonin agonist and the opiate blocker naltrexone, he has successfully remained sober for the last five months, not taken any opiates since the detoxification. Although he did fixate on some Vicodin he saw at a party, he decided not to take it. He can't explain why he feels the way he does. It is as if he just broke up with a girlfriend (opiates) and cannot get over the good feeling that he had when he was with her.

Trying to get rid of opiate cravings is an issue faced by many young men and women who have been on highly euphoric opiate drugs such as OxyContin. Using naltrexone, a competitive inhibitor that blocks the opiate receptors, has proven quite helpful in many cases. However, when treating opiate-dependent patients, their genetics and the other neurotransmitter systems must be taken into consideration because all neurochemical systems talk to each other. Given that Steven is a genetic alcoholic and alcohol affects many neurotransmitter systems, we can see that using a serotonin agonist and naltrexone to tend to the serotonin and opiate systems is not enough. We decided to add Wellbutrin to his list of medications, which increases dopamine, noradrenaline, and acetylcholine. Raising these neurochemicals in addition to serotonin has successfully helped curb opiate cravings in other cases of cross-addicted opiate-using genetic alcoholics.

Common Treatment for Opiate Addicts

The most common approach to detoxifying patients off of heavy narcotics is through the front door method. Medical professionals use different opiates like fentanyl or methadone to stimulate the opiate sites, and then try to titrate the system down. They also gradually decrease whatever medications the patient was taking, like Vicodin or Norco, on a daily basis. This slow method will cause the patient to stay in withdrawal for weeks or months while titrating the drugs down. This method disturbs all the other interconnected neurotransmitter systems, and it is a hard way to detoxify someone.

The opiate system could be described as the central axis of all the other seven systems – noradrenaline, dopamine, glutamate, GABA, endocannabinoid, acetylcholine, and serotonin. All these systems communicate amongst themselves, but the opiate system is the most domineering. Often doctors do not take into consideration the other systems they might be affecting while administering the medications. So they just treat the opiate system issue, ignoring the other systems entirely. I have a hard time accepting that approach. We take a history and physical of each patient, asking about past drug use and their family history to try and get a feel for their innate neurochemical balances. One of the first things we inquire about is whether or not the patient's parents were alcoholic. We then find out how and why they started taking opiates. Many patients start down the path of narcotics and find that they cannot stop for fear they will go into acute withdrawal without them.

Suboxone and Subutex are prescription medications that are currently being used by addictionologists and detoxification doctors throughout Europe and the United States. Many chemical dependency units today will send opiate-addicted patients home with simply a prescription for Suboxone or Subutex to detoxify them. Using these medications is another example of using the front door method to treat opiate addicts. Basically there are two parts to these medications. There is the buprenorphine, which directly hits the receptor sites of the opiate system, and there is the second product, a molecule that hovers around the receptor sites so that the buprenorphine cannot hit the opiate receptor sites directly. These kinds of medications are called *competitive inhibitors*. So by administering these kinds of drugs, they are creating a competition for the site and causing a relative withdrawal of the opiate system while at the same time stimulating it. I equate it to driving a Corvette 120 mph with the gas pedal all the way down and then pulling back on the emergency brake, causing smoke to come out the back of the car. That is essentially what doctors are doing to the opiate systems of patients – hitting the gas and the brakes at the same time. These medications stimulate opiate receptors while at the same time up-regulating the system. That method is costly.

The front door method is more often than not, effective, but it prolongs the withdrawal. I am in a situation where insurance companies give me only three or four days to get patients detoxified in the hospital. Unfortunately I have seen the Suboxone and Subutex fail, so my experience is skewed toward that approach. Quite frankly, it seems ethically wrong to have someone suffer for an extended period of time while going through the painstakingly slow withdrawal process of tapering off opiates. On the contrary, the best thing to do is to modify the system without having significant detoxification symptomatology over time. To do this you must utilize the other systems that the opiate system feeds into. A simple rule of thumb to follow is – *do not* taper someone off opiates unless they are taking the equivalent of less than five Vicodin per day.

Use the GABA System

There are other ways to safely stimulate the opiate system without knocking on the front door. We call these alternative ways, the *back door method*. There are seven other neurotransmitter systems surrounding and connected to the opiate system, and GABA has proven to be the most effective. Over the course of 20,000 detoxifications, we have observed that people using heavy GABA drugs seem to detoxify off opiates in a very mild and tolerable manner. For example, people who have entered the detoxification unit while still taking Valium products, phenobarbital, or other GABA-like drugs seem to detoxify more easily. In fact, in my detoxification unit, we have completely stopped using Suboxone, Subutex, and any other drug that directly hits opiate receptor sites. Instead, I am more than satisfied with the quick detoxification that results from using GABA drugs. This back door method to detoxification usually only takes a mere four to five days, as opposed to the front door method which can take months.

Even in the most extreme cases of opiate addiction, I still use the back door method. When I have a patient come in with three fentanyl patches, and taking #15 OxyContin, #50 Norco, and 200 mg of methadone a day, or any other combination of opiates, the first step we will always take is to stop the drugs immediately. We remove the patches and scrub the area with soap and water to make sure there is no direct effect of opiate receptor site activation by exogenous drugs or pills. This will cause them to go into acute opiate withdrawal, so we immediately stimulate the GABA system, which will in turn back-feed into the opiate system.

It is surprising just how well the GABA system works in up-regulating the opiate system. There are five known GABA receptor sites. At the GABA1a receptor site we can use short-term Valium-like products or benzodiazepines. However, I have found the most effective option is to utilize the other four receptor sites that often go unused. On the first day of the detoxification, we activate all four of these sites with various drugs and continue them for one month or more, except for the GABA site that phenobarbital acts on. Phenobarbital hits GABA sites that in turn talk to the opiate system and up-regulates it. People in acute opiate withdrawal have an increased amount of liver activation; therefore their liver will essentially grind up or metabolize those phenobarbital pills in 30 minutes. The opiate system drives the liver into hyperdrive like a wood chipper chipping away at all drugs. We can give someone in opiate withdrawal 30mg or 60mg of phenobarbital and it will last for only an hour, whereas normally it should last for 100 hours. To insure that the phenobarbital dosage remains at safe levels, we check them often, making sure they do not reach toxic levels. We can usually continue this high dosage without any ill side effects for sometimes up to four days. The liver is usually eating it up so fast that the phenobarbital levels are essentially nonexistent.

The opiate system returns to its proper balance approximately 72 to 80 hours after the detoxification began. At this point the liver comes out of hyperdrive and stops its rapid metabolizing of the phenobarbital. If high doses of phenobarbital continue to be administered past the 72 to 80 hour mark, the patient's phenobarbital level will go sky high, causing toxicity. In our thousands of detoxifications, this has only happened once, proving that using phenobarbital to detoxify patients off of opiates works, however it can only be used for a minimal amount of time. We do not give phenobarbital for more than five or six days. On the other hand, we continue to use GABA-like drugs and glutamate inhibitors like Neurontin, gabapentin, Robaxin, and sometimes Lyrica for a GABA effect that will target the other three receptor sites of the GABA system for up to a month or more.

Lately baclofen has proven to be an effective heavy GABA drug in detoxifying patients off opiates. It too back-feeds into the opiate system, and appears to be non-addictive. With all my years of experience in the detoxification unit, I consider something addictive if we have had to detoxify someone off the drug in the past. We have never had to detoxify someone off of baclofen, nor have we detoxified anyone off of Benadryl, trazodone, or Seroquel. Baclofen is a heavy GABA drug that really works wonders on the opiate system. It is also used to increase GABA for alcoholics. According to studies with alcoholics, baclofen's significant GABA effect decreases the chances of a drinking relapse. However, just because a medication is non-addictive, does not mean you should not take precautions when using it.

Taking baclofen for an extended period of time carries some risk. If that patient were to suddenly stop taking it, their GABA would rapidly drop. This, in combination with elevated glutamate or noradrenaline, could cause a person to have a grand mal seizure. So remember to be careful with the baclofen; do not use it for more than three weeks. The patient should take 200mg of Tegretol twice a day for several weeks after that, just to ensure that the patient does not go through withdrawal from baclofen or have a grand mal seizure. In addition to having a slight opiate effect, 200 mg of Tegretol twice a day works as an antiseizure drug that hits the GABA system at a different receptor site than baclofen. If baclofen is used for an extended amount of time, it must be slowly titrated.

Getting Patients with Pain Control Issues Back on their Natural Opiates

Often times after people go through many painful procedures, they get so used to their pain medications that they fear the consequences of going off the narcotics and end up taking opiates and benzodiazepines for years. Many start taking the opiate-activating medication to alleviate the pain from an acute back injury or some sort of surgery that caused long-lasting inflammation and muscle spasms. They develop a tolerance to the drugs and do not stop taking them because they are trying to stay one step ahead of withdrawal. They then use the drug just to prevent detoxifying on their own. Of course over that period of time, a lot of healing in their muscles has occurred, yet they cannot discern whether they still have the pain from the injury or if the pain that remains is just from withdrawal.

Patients with pain control issues are assured that using the GABA system to detoxify and reduce pain is most effective. In fact, our detoxification unit has been accredited with having superior standards and has been described as "miraculous" because we have been able to help all chronic pain patients who come into our unit without any selectivity at all. We have assisted patients with multiple back surgeries, pancreatitis, migraines, and numerous other chronic pain conditions. Of the 10,000 detoxifications off of opiates that we have performed on patients with pain issues, at least 85 percent of them have either the same or less pain than when they were on the opiates. While we utilize the GABA system to talk to the opiate system, we also use Lidoderm patches, some non-addictive muscle relaxants, and nerve pills such as Neurontin or Lyrica to decrease the spontaneity and activation of nerves in the legs, back, and so on. Once the opiate system is detoxified and all the exogenous opiates are removed from the body, the patient's own beta-endorphin will come back. The body's receptor sites will up-regulate, start functioning again, and be activated by the patient's natural beta-endorphin – the strongest opiate in the world.

Treating Underlying Disorders of Genetic Alcoholic Opiate Addicts

When treating opiate addicts who do not have pain management problems, it is most likely that they are cross-addicted genetic alcoholics, so their treatment must address that underlining deficiency. These kinds of opiate-addicts use the opiate system to decrease their cravings and modulate their levels of the neurotransmitters that alcohol would normally raise. One of the most frequent mistakes made in the detoxification field is using Suboxone to treat the opiate abusers who are in fact genetic alcoholics. As mentioned earlier, using Suboxone is the front door method to controlling the withdrawal symptoms that the patient has. Doctors use this agonistic approach to stimulate the opiate system, and then slowly titrate the Suboxone. Occasionally this works well to get the patient off high-dose narcotics like Norco, heroin, or methadone, unless of course the patient is a genetic alcoholic.

Genetic alcoholics should not be given Suboxone to treat their opiate addiction. Most addictionologists and chemical dependency units just focus on the opiate system when treating opiate addicts, not even taking into consideration whether they are genetic alcoholics or not. Doctors who do not probe into their patients' past and family history of their patients often do not find out that their patient is in fact a genetic alcoholic until it is too late. At first when an addictionologist places a patient on Suboxone, they are hitting the opiate system and satisfying the needs of the inherently deficient alcohol system. Their cravings are suppressed; the patient is feeling good about their recovery, until the Suboxone gets titrated down too far. That is when the real problem surfaces. They crave alcohol (if the patient ever used it in the past) because the alcohol system's neurotransmitters are no longer being effectively stimulated. So once the Suboxone is decreased past a certain level, the stimulation is no longer enough and the cross-addicted alcoholic will start drinking again. It can be quite alarming for the addictionologist to find that his opiate-addicted patient is in reality an alcoholic that is now drinking high doses of alcohol.

Cross-addiction with opiates and alcohol demonstrates that there is a strong relationship between the opiate system and the other neurotransmitter systems that alcohol raises. The alcohol system and the opiate system respond to one another and are very closely tied. Gradually titrating Suboxone down creates a neurochemical imbalance. Recall one of the first rules ever mentioned in this book – a neurochemical imbalance is a prerequisite for cravings. Slowly decreasing a patient's opiates causes the other neurotransmitter systems comprising the alcohol system to decrease, thereby initiating a craving for alcohol and ultimately a relapse. Therefore, one must treat the underlying genetic abnormalities to decrease cravings, in an effort to also treat the opiate system. Not only do we need to detoxify genetic alcoholic opiate-addicts off opiates, we also need to stop their cravings. To do this, we must fix the neurotransmitter deficiencies that alcohol momentarily alleviates.

Always remember that all of the neurotransmitter systems are connected and talk to one another and most alcoholics and drug addicts are born with deficiencies in their neurotransmitter levels. As addictionologists, we must get to the heart of our patients' cravings. My current methodology and knowledge of these neurochemical systems allows me to do just that. As we can see from the use of Suboxone, only treating the opiate system's down-regulation is ineffective because the patient will likely go back to either drinking or using opiates again. Genetic alcoholics who are cross-addicted to opiates must be detoxified with an agonistic or stimulating approach to the other five neurochemical systems that alcohol increases. Using a combination of a serotonin stimulant, a GABA and glutamate modulator, possibly a dopamine stimulant, and an opiate blocker usually does the trick and is necessary to prevent any future relapses.

When detoxifying cross-addicted genetic alcoholics, the first step is always to discontinue all opiates. This puts the opiate system and the other five neurotransmitter systems in the alcohol system out of balance again. So what do we do? We treat those five systems that genetics has rendered insufficient, because if the patient suddenly starts to crave alcohol, the easiest thing to reach for is an opiate; therefore, it is vital to balance out the other systems to avoid relapse. We use Campral to decrease glutamate and cravings. We raise patients' serotonin with Lexapro, Paxil, or Prozac. We might try to stimulate the dopamine system as well with Abilify or Wellbutrin. We can usually determine if they are deficient in dopamine by looking at their history of drug use. If they were ever blackout drinkers or used methamphetamine or cocaine, they likely have some dopamine deficiency. Addressing these other systems in our treatment has worked well for us in the detoxification unit. Cross-addicted patients treated with these methods of balancing out all of their neurotransmitter systems do not go back to using alcohol and are largely rid of their cravings for opiates.

Opiates, GABA, and Dopamine

One of the effects that makes taking high-dose opiates so addictive is the increased amount of dopamine released in the brain. Dopamine is actually a key player in both alcoholism and opiate abuse. That great feeling from the dopamine surge (which takes place in the ventral tegmental area of the cortico-mesolimbic) is what both opiate abusers and blackout drinkers alike are addicted to. Incidentally, to get that effect, the opiate system must first go through the GABA system for the dopamine system to be stimulated. Recent research appears to indicate that a chain reaction occurs among the opiate, GABA, and dopamine systems. The initial stimulation of the opiate receptor sites received from narcotics or alcohol sparks the release of GABA, which in turn ignites a surge of dopamine. What does all this mean when it comes to detoxifying patients off of opiates? Because of this threefold connection, opiate abusers in withdrawal actually become dopamine deficient, causing them to have a lot of anxiety and to feel horrible. For effective treatment, we take this into consideration when using GABA drugs. GABA in itself is calming, and it also energizes the dopamine system. So in a way, we side-step the opiates, getting the same dopamine effect in a safer manner, without abusing any kind of narcotic.

Dopamine receptor sites can become down-regulated because of excess swarming as result of heavy alcohol abuse, dopamine (i.e. cocaine) abuse, or even opiate abuse. Nevertheless, there are a number of prescription drugs out there to combat this dopamine down-regulation. Some of the most effective ones are actually opiate suppressors or competitive inhibitors such as naltrexone and Vivitrol. Prior to understanding the recent research on the threefold connection that exists between the opiate, GABA, and dopamine systems, it was always quite confounding to me that the cravings of a blackout alcoholic who seeks a dopamine surge when drinking, could be controlled with a drug that blocks the opiate system. Now we know what is actually happening.

Once a patient is sober and on an opiate-blocker medication,

Opiate-Abuser

Alcoholic/Blackout Drinker

Both opiate abusers and alcoholics who are blackout drinkers seek the euphoric high associated with the ultimate dopamine surge.

not only is the opiate system being blocked, the surging dopamine also becomes blocked. Suddenly the receptor sites that have been suppressed due to constant swarming and over-stimulation (because of the alcohol or opiates) have a chance to up-regulate and proliferate. With the patient now on opiate blockers such as naltrexone or Vivitrol, the patient's own natural D2 begins to proliferate, bringing their dopamine to a proper balance, making the patient feel happy again. At this point the patient no longer experiences cravings for alcohol or opiates. This effect of opiate blockers has been substantiated and proven by various studies on dopamine. It is important to understand that just as the methods of opiate detoxification that I employ focus on getting patients off narcotics and back on their own natural endogenous opiates, when it comes to getting people sober (whether off of opiates or alcohol), we use the medications that will actually increase the patient's own dopamine production.

Summary of Treating Opiate Addicts

I am not in favor of any type of Suboxone or Subutex use because using medications that directly stimulate the opiate system causes unpredictable results with the other neurotransmitter systems. Aside from affecting the other neurotransmitter systems, opiate use also affects other functions of the brain such as memory, which carry their own safety issues. Sending patients home on Suboxone for them to slowly detoxify on their own can be dangerous. Like any other opiates, it can seriously skew their brain's way of processing information. As noted in chapter 9, images are formed and placed in our temporal lobe as memories, and if one has skewed or partial memories because of the opiates they are on, they are working with flawed data to propel themselves through life and negotiate future conflicts.

I am a strong advocate of the more advanced method: stopping all opiate drugs, letting the system find its balance, assisting the patient through the withdrawal by stimulating the GABA system, and then decreasing the GABA drugs gradually over the course of one month. I believe that someday the current number one method of detoxifying patients off of opiates by using other opiates like Suboxone and Subutex, will lose favor. Once detoxification specialists see all the benefits to taking the more natural approach of using the GABA system, this will become the preferred way to detoxify patients. It is quicker, more efficient, and results in less suffering for the patient. This is clearly the best method to use. Why? Patients who have been detoxified by both methods return to us stating that the back door method was best and easier for them.

Brain Rules

Rule #52: If you want a fast detoxification, *do not* taper someone off opiates unless they are taking the equivalent of five or less Vicodin per day because that method is not always effective and it prolongs the symptoms of withdrawal. Instead, use the back door method.

Rule #53: The first step to almost any good opiate detoxification is to stop all opiate drug administration and begin heavy stimulation of the GABA system. This is my preference.

Rule #54: The alcohol system and the opiate system respond to one another and are very closely tied. Since they are all connected, using opiate stimulants like Suboxone when treating opiate addicts causes a neurochemical imbalance, not only in the opiate system, but also in the other systems.

Rule #55: Because the Opiate and GABA systems are uniquely married, it is easy to manipulate one and get a predictable response from the other.

Rule #56: Patients using heavy GABA drugs seem to detoxify off opiates in a very tolerable and mild manner. That is because up-regulation of the opiate system is one of the side-effects of GABA stimulation.

Rule #57: When treating patients with pain control issues, the key goal is to let their opiate system up-regulate and get their beta-endorphins working again. This goal can be attained through use of the back door method, where all opiates and benzodiazepines are discontinued, and other GABA drugs are used to stimulate the opiate system, bringing it to its proper balance.

Rule #58: When detoxifying genetic alcoholics who are cross-addicted to opiates, we must take an agonistic approach to the other five systems within the alcohol system. Usually a combination of a serotonin stimulant, GABA and glutamate modulators, a dopamine stimulant, and an opiate blocker is successful at both detoxifying the patient and preventing any relapse.

Rule #59: There is a threefold connection between the opiate, GABA, and dopamine systems. Because of this connection, opiate abusers in withdrawal actually become dopamine deficient, leading to added anxiety and discomfort. GABA drugs and opiate competitive inhibitors both work to combat these symptoms.

"Helping patients to understand the medical reasons behind their conditions does wonders to a patient's confidence and outlook. Somehow, knowing that the source of their affliction is likely neurochemical and the result of their genetic inheritance provides them with a great deal of comfort and hope."

Chapter 13

The Future of
Chemical Dependency Treatment

Congratulations! You now know more about the eight basic neurotransmitter systems than most doctors. Knowing these neurotransmitters and how they are interconnected is vital to both receiving and administering safe treatment. As a doctor, it is a good idea to keep up to date on what medications affect which neurotransmitters. It is always advantageous for both medical staff and patients to be informed. For patients receiving any kind of medication that affects neurotransmitters, remember – your health is your responsibility. If you know you have a predisposition toward addiction to certain kinds of medications, whether valium products, opiates, or any other kind of drug, you must take action. Know what your doctor is prescribing and know how much, in order to protect yourself against relapse. As for both doctors and patients, if you do not know which neurotransmitters a drug affects, find out, and do not forget to consider any underlying connections that could otherwise reap surprising results. The brain is a fine-tuned instrument; do your utmost to protect it.

Of all the neurotransmitter systems, the GABA and dopamine systems are the most intriguing and useful for detoxification specialists. GABA in particular is the most responsive to the needs of an addictionologist and others in the healthcare field. It is found throughout the brain, and just like any other neurotransmitter, some people are born with a lot of it and others are not. Since I was born with very little of this neurochemical, I have the extra energy to multitask at almost every moment of my life, but it also gets me into trouble. I talk too fast and have excess anxiety.

Regardless of the blessings and maledictions associated with little or excess neurotransmitters, whatever our genetic inheritance, we learn to deal with what we are given. However, sometimes the consequences of our neurotransmitter balances go beyond our control, and we turn to the consultation of doctors and psychiatrists to help us gain some power over our lives. Rightly so, we count on our doctors to be up to date, knowing all the latest and most effective treatment methods. The old method of psychiatrists and physicians making a DSM diagnosis on someone and then guessing at or picking a drug of choice to solve the problem will eventually be a thing of the past. Science holds the bright prospect of genetic testing to solve patients' problems in the future. Until then, we have this step in between – the method I have outlined in this book.

Know Your GABA:
Use the Other Sites

In my practice, I use GABA the most, so I often inform people of its useful properties. There are important details that you need to know about the GABA system in order to get optimal results. Not too long ago, I gave a lecture before university psychiatrists and asked if anyone knew how many types of GABA receptor sites we are currently aware of. No one in the room knew that at present there are at least five, maybe six, known GABA sites. So why do we need to know that there are all these GABA sites? Because not knowing is in part the source of our society's problem with over-prescribing. Not knowing leads to erroneous prescribing of drugs that negatively impacts people's lives. Knowledge is power. If you know that there are other GABA sites to hit, then you know there must be other drugs, other methods and options besides benzodiazepines and phenobarbital.

After reading this book, I do not need to tell you that the GABA1a site is highly addictive and often abused in today's society with all the benzodiazepine drugs and sleeping medications that are being prescribed. Burdening this site with over-stimulation leads to a paradoxical effect. Once patients' GABA1a sites get inundated with enough benzodiazepines for them to gain tolerance, they actually end up experiencing more agitation than they started with. This agitation comes from the glutamate system which is left virtually unopposed once the GABA1a sites have become disabled. Furthermore, if the GABA1a stimulating drug is stopped after tolerance is built, the glutamate is then completely unopposed and could possibly lead to a grand mal seizure. Keen medical assistance is required for these kinds of cases.

Recently, I admitted a college graduate who has had a sleeping disorder most of her life. She had been taking Ambien, a GABA drug, but stopped on her own because she felt ashamed of taking fifteen of these pills a day. The result: within several days of stopping the drug, she had two grand mal seizures because her glutamate was so high, relative to her suppressed GABA. She was left with insomnia and anxiety and a need for detoxification.

A doctor or psychiatrist not familiar with the five different receptor sites in the GABA system would likely put this patient on a different benzodiazepine drug which would then be slowly titrated down. This could lead to yet another grand mal seizure. Other physicians may put her on phenobarbital for a long time and then try to take her off of that, which could also very likely lead to a grand mal seizure. Phenobarbital successfully activates one of the other GABA sites, but it must be used with caution because of its addictive properties. Some find that the phenobarbital acts for a longer duration than benzodiazepine, while the benzodiazepine GABA1a site is more "punctual" or rapid acting. Benzodiazepines and phenobarbital definitely have their place in treatment, but it is the methods of their use that is in need of reform. Medical personnel are in a sense stuck on the GABA1a site or on phenobarbital's site because they do not know that there are other options.

Most physicians, psychiatrists, and even addictionologists do not know that if they forgo the stimulation of both the benzodi-azepine and phenobarbital sites, they can still get a tremendous GABA effect by stimulating the other three sites, slowing down the brain. While in the above-mentioned case we did give the patient phenobarbital for a limited amount of time just to get her through the roughest part of detoxification, once she was discharged and sent home, we utilized those other three GABA sites.

There is a lot of controversy in the research of the GABA system as to what other GABA drugs there are exactly. That is why you may have noticed that I refer to some drugs that stimulate the GABA system as *GABA drugs* and others as *GABA-like drugs*. For instance, Neurontin is considered GABA-like, even though it is not exactly GABA. Though Neurontin influences other neurochemicals, its effects of inhibiting the agitating glutamate means the end result is GABA-like. Recall that GABA is like the brake pedal to a car and glutamate is the gas pedal; Neurontin works by taking the foot off the accelerator, leaving the GABA breaks on and making the car come to a halt. Almost all drugs in one way or another affect GABA and/or serotonin in an indirect way. Some of those drugs are Robaxin, BuSpar (even though it is a 5-HT drug), Tegretol, and Topamax.

So, I ask, why not go to a different site? One does not need to continually bombard the GABA1a site or phenobarbital sites with GABA drugs. There are other less-obvious ways to get the calming effects of GABA. The other three sites in the GABA system all greatly stimulate GABA production, thereby safely raising GABA levels.

What is even more interesting is the fact that the other sites in the GABA system have thus far proven to be non-addictive.

Lack of knowledge about these other sites is what is killing patients' GABA systems, their ability to fight anxiety, their ability to stay calm, and their ability to reach a state of clarity and tranquility. Readily utilizing these other three sites is part of the bright future of chemical dependency treatment. In the last conference I had with a university psychiatrist, he wanted to know how to get someone off of ten benzodiazepine Xanax pills a day and not have a grand mal seizure. I told him to use the other sites. "Hit those other sites with reinforced medications, and that patient will leave the detoxification unit calmer than when he was on the high-dose benzodiazepines," I told him. He had troubles believing what I was telling him, but it is true. I regularly see the effects of the GABA system in all five of its receptor sites, and it is a *dramatic* effect. I cannot emphasize enough how vital it is to use the other four sites. There is absolutely no need to continuously hit an unpredictable GABA1a receptor site that is notorious for causing more anxiety, more psychological problems, and grand mal seizure activity.

Dopamine and Chemical Dependency:
Why the Future of Dopaminergic Medications is so Important to the Field of Detoxification and Neurochemistry

Understanding the connections that exist among the eight neurotransmitter systems is paramount to figuring out solutions to the vast array of chemical dependency problems that exist in our society. Dopamine and its connection to both alcohol and opiate abuse are gaining more and more attention with researchers and doctors everywhere. They are finding that dopamine release is actually a large part of what makes both opiates and alcohol so addictive.

While some chemical dependency problems are completely self-induced and others come about because of genetic neurochemical imbalances, still others occur because of the miscalculation of prescribed medications. On a daily basis you can find news reports on deaths that result from opiate drugs like OxyContin. The problems surrounding opiate drug abuse are growing, yet ironically there continues to be an increase in the amount of opiates prescribed. More and more doctors prescribe medications like Vicodin, Norco, and OxyContin even though there is a lot of addiction and death that result from those drugs. So what exactly do the other neurotransmitter systems like dopamine have to do with this opiate epidemic?

I believe the solution to the problems resulting from the overprescription of opiates lies in dopamine. Let me explain why. Opiates like OxyContin, Vicodin, and heroin stimulate the GABA system along with the opiate system, and eventually end up causing a euphoric dopamine surge. That surge is highly addictive and if reached with enough frequency, causes tolerance to build and the dopamine system to down-regulate. A huge part of the problem with opiates is actually the dopamine dependency that results from the high intake of opiates and the depression that often follows. Patients taking a lot of opiates are developing significant dopamine dependency and then they end up using the opiates to treat the accompanying depression. When patients come off of opiates, they actually crave more dopamine, because of the down-regulation that has occurred in that system. To treat the remaining dopamine deficiency that results from opiate use, we must look to medications that directly affect the dopamine system.

Unfortunately we only have a couple of dopamine-type drugs available. Recall, there are at least four different types of dopamine that our brain produces: D1, D2, D3, D4, and D5. Methamphetamine increases D1 and some D2. Cocaine raises D2 and some D3. Very little is known about D3. High levels of D4 cause schizophrenic and schizoaffective disorders. There are medications that inhibit D4 to treat that. Wellbutrin is somewhat of a weak dopaminergic drug, also hitting acetylcholine and noradrenaline receptors, but it does stimulate some dopamine receptors. I am not sure whether it hits D1, D2, or D3, but I am pretty sure it does not hit D2 receptor sites because it does not make schizophrenics any worse. I suspect it is a partial D1 and D2 drug. Abilify is specifically a D2 drug and recent findings suggest that it decreases cravings for methamphetamine and cocaine.

High dopamine levels, whether induced by cocaine, methamphetamine, or the opiate system, are highly addictive and are driving individuals into despair with a silent disruption and costs that are staggering. Whatever the initial cause, more and more people are dying trying to satisfy their need for more dopamine, whether they use illicit dopamine drugs or opiates to get that desired surge. I actually believe there are more deaths that result from people trying to stimulate their dopamine system with opiates than those trying to stimulate their dopamine system with dopaminergic drugs like cocaine and methamphetamines.

Not knowing about this underlying connection between opiates and the dopamine system has doctors, pharmaceutical companies, and the government somewhat fooled. When they hear about the epidemic of opiate abuse, they only focus on the opiates alone, not understanding that these drugs drive dopamine. They are missing the piece to the puzzle that explains, **opiate addiction leads to a dopamine deficiency.** Patients who have unknowingly been using increasing amounts of opiates to assuage their dopamine deficiency would in fact benefit from other dopaminergic medications. Of course, it takes three or four weeks after detoxifying for the patient's dopamine to increase and get to a level where they are not over-emotional and crying with completely fragmented personalities due to the dopamine deficiency. Doctors tend to want to treat everybody with opiates like Suboxone and Subutex. By taking this route of using other opiates, they end up increasing dopamine and making the patients just as dependent as they were while on the other opiates.

On the contrary, using such drugs as naltrexone seems to work wonders for detoxifying alcoholics and opiate abusers. It works by inhibiting the opiate and dopamine release in the nucleus accumbens. This allows these systems to up-regulate, permitting the dopamine receptor sites to then proliferate. Now with all these dopamine receptors restored and fully functioning, patients need dopamine to hit those sites. That is why using naltrexone with Abilify or buproprion does great at improving the condition of patients who were on alcohol, have depression, and/or have used opiates in the past.

Dopamine, that is where the money is; that is where the success is. That is also where the treatment for individuals coming off opiates should be focused. It would be of great help if the pharmaceutical industry could identify new D1, D2, and D3 drugs, as well as new D4 inhibitors. It would save a lot of chemically dependent patients from future cravings and relapse.

Genetics' Potential for Future Chemical Dependency Treatment

Just the other day, I discussed with a psychiatric pharmacist how genetic testing and evaluation of the genome would affect the future of prescribing psychiatric medications. Psychiatrists today are very intuitive in their methods of prescribing. While they listen to patients describe their symptoms and observe their reactions to certain types of questions, they examine their patients for mood disorders, behavioral disorders, and cognitive ability. Psychiatrists know what drugs generally work for which kinds of patients, and that is how they choose what to prescribe.

Now, can you imagine a patient going in for a doctor's visit and getting a DNA test done, where a computer analyzes the DNA and then determines how much and what type of drug or drugs the patient should take? Whether this is good or bad, I believe that is where the future lies. A number of companies are interested in creating genetic tests for various diseases such as schizophrenia, bipolar disorder, depression, breast cancer, and so on. We are finding more and more sequences in the genetic code that are consistently tied to diseases that affect many people today.

We know there are 60 billion nucleotides and that alcohol may affect at least 120 polymorphisms. The gene 2q35 has some characteristics of possible genetically endowed alcoholism. We know about the upper end of the 13th chromosome and how that affects opiate dependency. One day we will be able to do genetic testing on a patient with depression, alcoholism, or a history of drug abuse, and find out exactly what deficiency exists and where it is located in the genome. We already know that the genome holds the instructions for how to make the brain. In the future, we will also be able to scientifically prove that the genome has an influence on the characteristics and the quantity of certain neurotransmitters in the brain.

I can just see it now – a patient goes to the doctor's office and gets a DNA test done for approximately $1,000. When he gets the results, he finds out which of the serotonins, dopamines, glutamate, or other neurochemicals of the brain are out of balance. Patients will be able to learn what imbalances, discrepancies in quantity, or overproduction of the neurotransmitters are causing their psychological and chemical dependency problems. Upon finding out which neurochemicals they are deficient in, patients will then find the medication that would best modulate those neurochemicals in a corrective way. That would be the best and most effective treatment scientifically that one could achieve. However, with all our scientific advancement, we are not there yet. So until then, we must rely on knowledge of the neurotransmitters, their interactions with one another and their reactions to external forces, in order to determine which medications are best for each individual's case. To assist individuals in doing that, I recommend using the diagram of the eight neurotransmitters that you have seen displayed throughout this book. The segment following this chapter will explain how to use it.

The Step in Between

While I am eagerly awaiting the kind of genetic testing that will reveal which parts of the genome or chromosomes are influencing the neurochemistry of the brain, until then, I will continue to inform patients and individuals in the medical field about the methodology I currently employ. This book has been written in a concise manner so that almost anyone can understand the neurotransmitter systems and be better equipped to help both others and themselves. This is the only book I know of that describes a methodology behind successfully determining which neurotransmitters are out of balance within patients; however, this is only the beginning. I have provided a firm foundation for people to start off with, but really, learning about the brain is an endless venture. I encourage you to do as I do and read PubMed often, in order to keep up to date with all the newest trends and findings. Doing so will enable you to continue fitting together the vast puzzle of the mind, its neurotransmitters and how those systems relate to one another.

There are definitely some difficult detoxification cases out there, and that is why having a method is so important. The methodology that I utilize daily has successfully helped thousands of people to over-come their addictions, leaving them happier and more confident. The most confusing cases are a challenge, not only for the families and the patients themselves, but also for physicians. Simply trying various medications until the right one is found, is no longer valid. There is no time for that. That approach can cause more harm than good, with patients becoming more depressed. In fact, it can be downright dangerous. There ought to be a scientific method to guide the prescribing of medications.

Physicians and psychiatrists need to look at the medications they prescribe from a neurochemical standpoint. Not doing this, leads to doctors frequently prescribing drugs that are in conflict with one another on a neurochemical level. Currently, not a day goes by that I do not see a patient receiving treatment from another doctor who has prescribed medications that are actually in conflict with one another. By changing those medications and taking note of how their various neurotransmitter systems have and will be affected, I have reaped outstanding results. Other physicians I have shared these methods with have tried it and had similar outcomes. They have been surprised to find just how simple, yet effective the methods I employ are.

While genetic testing has not yet reached its full potential in the field of chemical dependency treatment, we do have this new method that takes into account individuals' genetic background. Applying this methodology allows you to find the right medication and treatment routes, eliminating guessing and the accompanying dangers that follow. Once physicians and psychiatrists have grasped some of the finer aspects of this method and can draw the diagram in front of the patient they are treating, and explain what they believe to be the neurochemical basis for that individual's problems, they have made a great advancement in the way they treat their patients.

Really, if you are in any field where your job is to treat people with behavioral disorders or addiction problems, it would behoove you to apply what you have learned in this book when you talk to your patients. If you draw out the neurotransmitter diagram and explain what is going on to your patient using the concepts I have described in this book, your patient will not only have more confidence in you as a fully competent health provider, but you will also help to put their mind at ease. Helping patients to understand the medical reasons behind their conditions does wonders to a patient's confidence and outlook. Somehow, knowing that the source of their affliction is likely neurochemical and the result of their genetic inheritance provides them with a great deal of comfort and hope.

Teaching patients about the root cause of their problems is humane, and to me, there is no better way to treat the ailing. Letting patients know that their feelings and emotions are legitimate provides a relief that is beyond compare. Informing patients of the source of their behavioral, mental, and addiction problems is a caring methodology and not a feel-good sham; rather, it is backed by science. Patients today are not dumb. They have the right to know the source of their problems just as much as, if not more than, their physicians. They want to be active, not passive, participants in their treatment. They are advocates of learning everything they can about their own medical care, working with the physician or psychiatrist to gain control over their feelings and actions, and to better their lives.

Brain Rules

Rule #60: The best long-term treatment for chemical dependency lies in prescribing the proper medication to address underlying neurochemical deficiencies and prevent cravings.

How to Visualize Patients' Neurotransmitter Systems–
Instructions on How to Use the Neurotransmitter Diagram

By now, you have learned a lot about neurotransmitters and how their levels are genetically predetermined. Likely you have noticed the diagram representing the eight basic neurotransmitter systems significant to chemical dependency placed throughout this book. Every time I speak with a chemically dependent patient, visualizing this diagram helps me to understand what is going on within his or her brain and how its neurochemical balance is influencing what he or she is experiencing. There are actually several helpful ways to utilize this diagram. I use this diagram when visualizing (1) any genetic deficiencies patients are trying to make up for by abusing drugs or alcohol, (2) how those drugs or alcohol are affecting their neurotransmitter levels, (3) how withdrawal and detoxification will alter their neurotransmitter levels, and (4) how medications have or *will* affect their balance of neurotransmitters. Whether you use one, a few, or all of these ways, these diagrams will help you to determine what the source of the patients' problems are and which medication(s) will work best at keeping their brain in proper balance.

Placing the Neurotransmitters

The neurotransmitter diagram is very helpful when analyzing a patient's neurochemical status. The large circle represents the patient's brain, while the eight smaller circles represent the eight neurotransmitter systems. When sketching the diagram, it is best to have the opiate circle in the middle, the serotonin at approximately one o'clock, the GABA between two and three o'clock, the glutamate between four and five o'clock, the dopamine at six o'clock, the noradrenaline between seven and eight o'clock, the acetylcholine between nine and ten o'clock, and the endocannabinoid at eleven o'clock.

By consistently placing these circles representing each of the neurotransmitters in the same locations when drawing out this diagram, there is no need to label them. You should always know, for

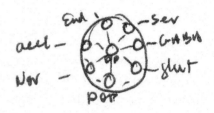

example, that dopamine is at the bottom, opiate is in the middle, GABA and glutamate are always next to each other, and so on. Their placement helps you to recall the associations that exist among them.

Diagram One: Showing the Genetic Ailment

After I have spoken with a new patient about his or her disposition, background, cravings, and any past or present drug use, the

An example of what the genetic diagram of a patient addicted to cocaine and suffering from depression might look like.

first thing I use the diagram to illustrate is what I perceive to be their genetic balance of neurotransmitters – too much of this, too little of that, and so on. This should reflect what their balance of neurotransmitters was prior to using any drugs. Once the diagram is drawn, write down next to it any over-all genetic predispositions that tend to run in the family such as alcoholism, bipolar disorder, schizophrenia, and so on.

Diagram Two: Demonstrating the Effects of Drug Abuse

The next thing I use the diagram to illustrate is how the drugs they currently are using are influencing their original genetic deficiencies or overabundance of neurochemicals. I write down any drugs that the patient uses or craves and draw arrows up or down

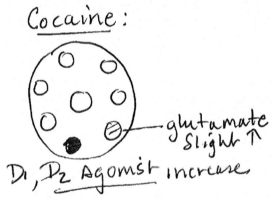

The effects of cocaine on the genetically depressed patient.

showing whether they stimulate or inhibit the production of each affected neurotransmitter. Generally you will find that the drugs the patient loves best are accounting for the neurotransmitters they are lacking. The actions of the drugs in this diagram will typically cancel out any imbalances found in the first diagram.

Diagram Three: Anticipating Withdrawal's Effects on Neurotransmitter Levels

Any neurochemical imbalance caused by drugs will lead to withdrawal if the use was significant enough to cause the down-regulation of their systems. In chemical dependency, what goes down

The effects of withdrawl once cocaine is discontinued

must come up. Withdrawal, the brain's method of up-regulation (returning the brain's neurochemical balance to its original genetic baseline), causes significant agitation and other unfavorable symptoms associated with detoxification. To represent this process on the third diagram, one might put big negative signs or one or two arrows pointing down near each circle that represents an affected neurotransmitter system. This is to help visualize what is going to take place once those drugs are stopped and the patient goes into withdrawal.

For example, this third diagram for a patient coming off opiates like heroin or OxyContin would show a decrease in GABA, dopamine, and opiates with arrows pointing downwards. For a patient coming off of alcohol, this diagram would show a decrease in serotonin, GABA, and dopamine, and an increase in glutamate, because these are the most strongly affected systems. A patient coming off of methamphetamine would have a diagram showing a drop in dopamine and norepinephrine. The diagram of a patient coming off of benzodiazepines will show extremely low GABA.

The actions on this diagram and the second one typically cancel each other out (looking like an intensified version of Diagram #1 because now, instead of having an agonistic effect from the drugs they are abusing, there is suddenly a marked deficiency. When people suddenly stop using an addictive drug, their deficiency in neurotransmitters can and usually will drop below their genetic baseline (which was illustrated in the first diagram).

If you understand everything thus far, you are doing quite well.

Looking at the three above-mentioned diagrams (their genetic endowment of neurotransmitter levels, the effects of the drugs they are taking on their neurotransmitter levels, and the effects of withdrawal on their neurotransmitter levels) can reveal a lot of interesting things. It can reveal possible underlying mental disorders.

Anticipating what a patient's neurochemical levels will be while in acute withdrawal is a big part of insuring that a detoxification progresses smoothly. Those who ignore the significance of neurotransmitter levels during and after detoxification are less effective in treating their patients. The drop in neurochemicals that occurs after the detoxification is complete is what prevents patients from staying off the drugs in the first place.

After drawing these first three diagrams for patients, you can figure out how to eliminate cravings once their drug(s) of choice is taken away. Recall that it takes three to four weeks for the neurochemicals to return to their normal levels. Once their detoxification is complete and they are stabilized, if their reason for doing the drugs in the first place was because of an underlying genetic deficiency in their neurotransmitter levels, their genetic predispositions will become evident. It is important to analyze this so you can take corrective measures with medications that will stop cravings before they even start.

Diagram Four: The Treatment Plan

The final application of this diagram is to visualize all corrective measures that will be taken. The fourth diagram shows the effects of any medications used to correct both the deficiencies that were shown on the diagram representing their genetic levels, and those that result from drug abuse and withdrawal. I call this the

A treatment diagram showing medications' effects when
remedying the patient's depression and cocaine addiction.

treatment diagram. We use this to plan our treatment for patients'
detoxifications, cravings, and any other disorder they may have, like
depression. By taking note on the diagram of all the effects that each
medication has on the patient's neurochemicals, any discrepancies
or overlying conflict between the effects of medications will also
become evident.

You can also use the diagram to discern the effects that any
medications or illicit drugs they used in the past had on their neurotransmitter systems. By taking note of where on this diagram they
were affected as well as any other side effects they had, one can gain
an integrated idea of what is good and what is bad for the patient.

Why Use These Diagrams?

By using these diagrams, one can clearly see which neurotransmitters' imbalances are influencing the patient's actions and which
neurotransmitters are having a significant impact on the patient's
drug use, mental status, and/or other neurotransmitter-influenced
inadequacies.

Prior to understanding how the neurotransmitters are such an
integral part of chemical dependency, I used to use intuition for
treating chemically dependent patients, hoping for a successful
outcome. Using this diagram to visualize the state of patients' neurotransmitter systems has greatly improved the quality and outcome
of my patients' treatment. However, in spite of its effectiveness,
there is no perfect stringent drug profile for each patient. As you
can see from all the diagrams attributed to each patient, things
can get quite complex, and no two patients are exactly the same.

That is why one must become adept at gathering information from each patient, finding out what their genetic makeup is and which drugs they desire, and which ones they had an adverse reaction to. Among other things, you also must find out when they last used the drug, how they feel, and what they are craving. If it seems like there are too many variables to consider when treating a chemically dependent person using this method and these diagrams, just imagine the alternative – jumping in without a plan and guessing what you should do.

I often get asked how we detoxify patients off multiple combinations of drugs in just four days and have them leave our detoxification unit on no addictive drugs or medications, and yet have them calmer, happier, and in less pain than when they were taking 20 or 30 pills per day. It seems impossible to others to get consistent results like that. I tell them it is this method that I employ. Because it is based on science as oppose to intuition, it almost never fails.

There are a few twists, but understanding and drawing out the systems is the only way to match the complex human brain and its dynamic predictable changes. Harnessing that predictability makes it a lot easier to get predictable results. I have never liked uncertainty. Business school teaches, when you face uncertainty, get more data. Making a decision when there is uncertainty will cost you dearly. Once more data is gathered, arrange the data into a coherent structure which is plausible. Evaluate the danger with the opportunity and set it into action, watching for change and positive results.

This method that I have taught you and these diagrams that you should learn to use are invaluable to the field of detoxification. If you are lost and confused at this point, do not lose hope. Working this system over and over again and drawing out the diagrams with every patient you encounter will help you to gain proficiency. You cannot attain proficiency just by reading a book; you need practice. Learn more about these neurotransmitter systems and start looking at medications and drugs in a new way. Do not simply look at the drug by name; look at its actions on the receptor sites of the neurotransmitter systems it affects. Do not stop there. Then think about the chain reaction that occurs throughout the other neurotransmitter systems, whether in a agonist or antagonist way.

The pharmaceutical manufacturers do not promote sales of their medications based on this system. They promote them on psychiatric diagnosis, not on how they work neurochemically. But there is nothing stopping you from asking. Sadly though, most drug representatives do not even know how they work. They are just taught enough to know what to say to make the sale. They rarely are informed on which neurotransmitters the drugs affect and the manner in which they do so. But it never hurts to find out and ask.

Diagram Synopsis

As a review, the first diagram of patients' neurotransmitter systems should reveal their genetic baseline profile of neurochemicals they were born with. It will probably reflect an imbalance with too little of this and too much of that. The second diagram shows what the drugs they are addicted to are doing to those neurotransmitter levels, stimulating or inhibiting and to what degree. The third diagram reveals how detoxification will then alter those neurochemical levels. The forth diagram discloses what will happen to the patients' neurochemical levels once we administer the medications that (1) will help them get through the withdrawal safely, (2) help rid them of any cravings they may have, and (3) correct any genetic imbalances that led to their addiction in the first place. The next segment will examine why anti-craving medications are so useful to the field of chemical dependency.

Using Medications to Stop Cravings
An Introduction to a Drug Index

I was recently confronted by a colleague who asked me if there was any justification for the medications that we prescribe to patients in detoxification and recovery. He inquired how it is I know which medications to continue and which to stop. He asked if there are any published findings that document the effectiveness of the medications our unit utilizes.

The best way to explain the justification behind my choices in medications was to contrast the results I get now using my current medication regimens, with those that I had gotten in the past. Our program used to be like any other detoxification unit, having a 50 percent success rate with half of all patients relapsing within a year. After detoxifying approximately 5,000 patients and having half of them relapse, I knew something was wrong with our program. There was clearly room for improvement, but it was as if we were missing a very important part of the puzzle. Over the course of several years of trying to decipher why so many people relapsed, I finally figured out it was the *focus* that was all wrong. Instead of just focusing on the detoxification process, we should have been looking at the root of the problem – cravings. People would detoxify, attend Alcoholics

Anonymous meetings or other support groups, and see physicians, yet a lot of them would still be craving alcohol or their other drugs of choice. I noticed that other patients who did not relapse were taking certain medications which they claimed eliminated their cravings. When those patients ran out of their medications because the prescription was not renewed, their cravings returned, relapse ensued, and they would need to be detoxified again.

After taking note of the importance of focusing on cravings, I began to recognize patterns and pay attention to which medications prevented which kinds of cravings. The detoxification unit where I have worked for twenty years is much like a laboratory where I have the opportunity to constantly observe and take note of the effects of various medications on the brain's neurochemicals. Not only that, the thousands of patients that have passed through there have taught me a lot about detoxification, relapse, and the heart of what *craving* is all about. By using medications to address patients' neurotransmitter deficiencies (those associated with alcoholism, drug abuse, and other psychiatric conditions) and put a halt to their cravings, the incidence of patients maintaining sobriety increased drastically. Firsthand experience in tandem with my continual research into all the latest discoveries surrounding neurochemicals and their relationships among each other has refined my understanding of how each drug affects these neurotransmitter systems. By considering the research of others as well as observing the effects of medications on my patients, I have been able to piece together a list of drugs that successfully suppresses patients' cravings. The National Institute of Drug Abuse (NIDA) has come out with a list of drugs that have proven effective in stopping cravings. These were in congruence with the medications that I have been using for the last five to ten years.

As for the results of using these anti-craving drugs, counselors and our research staff revealed that 85 percent of the people whom we had detoxified, treated, and placed on various anti-craving medications did not return to our unit in one year (a striking improvement from a previous average of 50 percent). The proof that the secret to the best long-term treatment for chemical dependency lies in prescribing the proper medications to address underlying deficiencies and thereby treat cravings is undeniable. Further evidence that has substantiated our choices in medications has come from simply observing and speaking with our patients – both those that do not relapse, and those that do. We have had patients return to us in the detoxification unit to tell us that they ran out of their medication, could not get them refilled for one reason or another, and within three or four days of their having stopped the medication, they relapsed. There is no coincidence there. For example, many people taking Topamax, the GABA drug, state they have *no* cravings. Individuals who have for months or even years been taking Campral, a glutamate adjuster, and experienced decreased cravings during that time, will relapse within three or four days of not taking it. People who take serotonin drugs to control their cravings have an even higher incidence of relapse once they stop taking their medications. Opiate blockers such as naltrexone and Vivitrol have been highly advantageous in preventing people from relapsing. Many of the medications that we have prescribed by serendipity have proven effective in treating alcoholism and drug addiction.

In summary, I told my questioning colleague to look at what was at stake. Though keeping a patient on these anti-craving medications may have a high cost, often times when the neurochemical imbalance is genetic, willpower is not enough to keep a patient out of the grips of relapse. It is important for physicians to bear in mind that the patient has a lot to lose if anti-craving medications are stopped and they slip into a relapse. Among other things, they could lose their family, job, driver's license, psychological status, as well as their self-confidence, self-identity and self-respect. One's entire life value could be lost due to the lack of a few prescribed medications that act to hold them together and prevent them from relapsing. True, there have been no extensive studies proving these medications infallible, but seeing how they work on a day to day basis with thousands of patients succeeding in living productive lives while taking these anti-craving medications is plenty of proof for me. Our success rate of 85 percent without relapse, has also strengthened our resolve to continue treating with these medications. We have had neither complications of cardiac arrest nor any major reactions to these medications, nor any type of psychological decomposition as result of taking them. We are constantly on the vigil, trying to make sure that that remains the case in our detoxification unit. Drug abuse and alcoholism are harmful not only to the addicted individual, but also to those around them. There is so much at stake in this venture of trying to stop the disease of alcoholism and drug addiction and its detrimental effects on society. Indeed we are on the frontier of neuroscience. Everyday further discoveries of the inter-workings of the brain are made. We must not be frightened away from advancement.

I have reviewed these efficacious medications, observed their effects, and questioned myself over and over again: "What am I doing? Is this right? How can this be? How can the results be *this* good? Is this too good to be true?" I cannot tell you how many times a month I review my own use of medication, treatment, and analysis, and still to this day I know that this is the best way to treat complex cases of patients with neurochemical problems and imbalances. No other method can match these results.

NOTE: The following is a list of drugs with their neurochemical agonistic and antagonistic effects listed beside them. Of course each drug has many additional complex effects, but this list solely focuses on the prevalent neurochemical effects. As always, all medications must absolutely be used with caution. The reader must understand that there is a high degree of variability between each individual's brain chemistry and their reactions to drugs. No two people will react in the exact same way to a medication even with identical dosages or routes of administration. **The following Drug Index is *not* a guide. It is a list *only* for interest and general understanding.**

Drug Index

Drug — Neurotransmitter Effect

Acetylcysteine — Restores Glutamate balance. Reduces cravings for Cocaine and Heroin

Alcohol — Serotonin (5HT3), GABA, Glutamate, Dopamine, Opiate, and Endocannabinoid agonist.

Ariprazole, Abilify — Dopamine agonist D2 (90% bound) 5HT1a agonist, 5HT2a antagonist

Aricept — Acetylcholine agonist

Cocaine — Dopamine Agonist D2, Possible D1 agonist

Cyclobenzapine (Flexeril) — Unknown effect

Cyproheptadine — Block H1 atropine like, Anti-Serotonin

Desipramine, Norpramine — Serotonin and Norepinephrine agonist

Desvenlafaxine, Pristiq — Serotonin and Norepinephrine agonist

Dexmethylphenidate, Focalin — Norepinephrine and Dopamine agonist, Amphetamine like

Dextroamphetamine Sulphate, Dexedrine — Norepinephrine and Dopamine agonist, Amphetamine, D1

Dextromethorphan — NMDA, Glutamate inhibitor. GABA-like effect

Diazepam, Valium — GABA1a site agonist. Unpredictable site.

Disufiram, Antebuse — Inhibits Aldehyde dehydrogenase. Small Dopamine agonist

Dolasetron, Zofran — Selective Serotonin inhibitor. 5HT3.

Dopamine Hcl — Drug used for Shock in ICU

Doxepin, Sinequan — Norepinephrine and Serotonin Agonist

Dronabinol, Marinol — Endocannabinoid Agonist

Duloxetine, Cymbalta — Norepinephrine and Serotonin agonist (reuptake inhibitor)

Escitalopram, Lexapro — Serotonin agonist, Seems to increase many 5HT's

Eszopiclone, Lunesta — GABA Drug

Fentanyl, Duragesic — Opioid agonist, Hard analgesic

Flumazenil, Romazicon — GABA1a site inhibitor, Competitive inhibition/antagonist.

Fluoxetine, Prozac — Serotonin agonist

Fluphenazine — Dopamine antagonist, Alpha adrenergic blocker.

Fluvoxamine, Luvox — Serotonin agonist, Weak Norepinephrine agonist

Gabapentin, Neurontin — GABA-like, glutamate inhibitor

Quanisetron, Kytril — Selective Serotonin inhibitor 5HT3

Haloperidol, Haldol — Dopamine antagonist, receptor blocker

Hydromorphone, Dilaudid — Opioid>GABA>Dopamine agonistic effect.

Hydroxazine, Vistaril — Histamine like blocker. True mechanism unknown

Ilopridone — Dopamine and Serotonin antagonist.

Imipramine — Norepinephrine, Serotonin and Acetylcholine agonist.

levetivacetram, Keppra — GABA like, Anti-epilepsy medication

Levorphenol, Levodromoran — Opioid>GABA>dopamine agonists

Lisdexampfetamine, Vyvanase — Norepinephrine and Dopamine (D1,D2) agonist. Amphetamine.

Lithium, Eskalith, Lithobid — Norephinephrine and Dopamine antagonist. Mechanism unknown.

Lorazepam, Ativan — GABA1a agonist. Benzodiazepine. Slows brain.

Loxapine, Loxitane — Dopamine antagonist. Schizophrenia>D3 inhibition?

Magnesium Sulphate — Binds to NMDA-Glutamate. Calming effect.

Maprotiline Hcl — Norepinephrine and Serotonin agonist.

Marijuana — Endocannabinoid agonist, CB1 and CB2 receptor sites.

Memantine, Namenda — NMDA antagonist. Alzheimer drug.

Methamphetamine — Dopamine and Norepinephrine agonist (D1,D2)

Meperidine, Demerol — Opioid>GABA>Dopamine agonist.

Methylphenidate, Ritalin — Noradrenergic and Dopamine agonist

Methadone — Opioid>GABA>Dopamine agonist

Midazolam — GABA1a agonist

Mirtazapine Remeron — Norepinephrine and Serotonin Antagonist

Modafanil, Provigil — Dopamine D1 agonist.

Molindone, Moban — Dopamine antagonist, antipsychotic

Morphine Sulphate — Opioid>GABA>Dopamine

Nabilone, — Cannabinoid agonist

Naloxone, Narcan — Opioid antagonist, Dopamine antagonist, Dopamine receptor agonist

Naltrexone, Revia — Opioid receptor antagonist, Dopamine antagonist, Increase Dopamine receptor sites

Nicotine — Acetylcholine, Norepinephrine and Dopamine agonist.

Nortriptyline — Norepinephrine and Serotonin agonist

Odansetron, Zofran — Selective Serotonin Inhibitor. 5HT3. Anti nausea, Opioid detox

Olanazpine — Dopamine, Serotonin, Histaminic1 antagonists

Oxcabazine, Trileptal — Unknown mechanism

Oxycontin, Oxycodone — Opioid>GABA>Dopamine agonist.

Paliperidone, Invega — Dopamine and Serotonin antagonist, alpha adrenergic blocker. Blocks H1

Paroxetine, Paxil — Serotonin agonist

Pentazocine, Talwin — Opioid agonist (Mu receptor) weak Serotonin and Norepinephrine agonist

Phenobarbital — GABA agonist

Phenelzine, Nardil — Norepinephrine and Serotonin agonist

Pregabalin — GABA-like agonist

Pranipexole, Mirapex — Dopamine receptor agonist

Prazocin, Minipress — Norepinephrine blocker, Alpha 1 Noradrenergic blocker. Amygdala blocker.

Ramelteon — Melatonin agonist

Risperidone, Risperidol — Dopamine and Serotonin antagonist

Saphris — Dopamine and 5HT2a antagonists

Sertaline, Zoloft — Serotonin agonist

Seroquel — Dopamine and Serotonin antagonists

Topiramate, Topamax — GABA agonist, Gluatamate antagonist, See Zonigran/Campral

Valproic Acid, Depakote — GABA-like activity, otherwise unknown

Venlafaxine, Effexor — Norepinephrine and Serotonin agonist, Some dopamine agonist

Ziprasidone, Geodon — Dopamine and Serotonin antagonism.
    Schizophrenia
Zolepion, Sonata — Nonbenzodiazepine hitting the GABA(A) site.
Zonegran — GABA agonist, Glutamate antagonist.

Note: This list of drugs and their neurochemical/neurotransmitter agonistic and antagonistic effects is written only for interest and general understanding. The medications listed here should only be used under the supervision of a certified medical professional and if used, need to be used with caution. Research has only partially expressed the varying effects of these medications, and there is still much to be learned. Aside from the effects listed here, there are definitely other complex effects which we have neither the space nor the time to express here. The reader must understand that there is a high degree of variability between one individual and the next. A drug that will have one effect on an individual's brain can vary substantially on someone else who has an entirely different assortment of neurochemical balances. No two people will react the same to the administration of a drug in the same dosage or route of administration. Thus, the reason this list is only for interest and general understanding. Due to rapid advances in research, new findings can alter the functions listed above, however this list was state of the art at the time of publishing.

Case Studies*

#1 Modafinil Detoxification

#2 Anticipating Neurotransmitter Reactions

#3 OxyContin Abuse

#4 Benzodiazepine and Opiate Detoxification of a Self-Medicating Bipolar Patient

#5 Benzodiazepine Withdrawal

#6 An Opiate and Alcohol Detoxification

#7 Bipolar Patient Addicted to Opiates

#8 A Genetic Alcoholic on Opiates

#9 Common Complications in the ICU

#10 Off the Ventilator and Extubated

#11 Acute Opiate Withdrawal in the Hospital

#12 Xanax and a GABA Deficiency

#13 Treating a Dopamine Deficiency

#14 The Unpredictable GABA1a Site

* All case studies included in this book are produced from generalities found in the field of chemical dependency. It is by chance and not by purpose if similarities between the fictional individuals in the case studies and the reader are found. There is no intent to identify or harm anyone with this narrative. The purpose of including these case studies in this manuscript is only to educate.

We published the author's own handwritten illustrations with the intent of showing how you can write them out spontaneously, free hand. We encourage you to do the same, this way, you can reveal your thoughts to others and have a record of your reasoning process and what you were thinking when you made the neurotransmitter analysis. It is amazing to see the response you get from the people you are working with, including the patients when you tell them what you think is wrong and what reason you have for implementing a particular action plan with them. That is the fun part, and you will be rewarded when people tell you how much sense it makes to them. This adds confidence in your approach.

Case Study #1
Modafinil Detoxification

Patient Profile: A 54-year-old working housewife had been having troubles staying awake during long shifts at work, so ten years ago she started taking modafinil (Provigil). She had also had some obsessive-compulsive traits, and increased her amount of modafinil through her psychiatric care. She is now up to 2400 mg of modafinil, taking twelve pills at 200mg throughout the day. She also takes twelve 1mg pills of lorazepam (Ativan) for anxiety and the D2 dopamine stimulant Abilify in small doses. Seeing the warning signs of high tolerance, her psychiatrist now wants her to stop taking modafinil. When the patient does this, she becomes hypersomnolent and anxious.

Drug Profile: Modafinil (Provigil) is an interesting neurochemical agonist. This highly effective stimulant drug was initially given to bomber pilots to keep them awake and alert as they flew from the United States to Afghanistan. That 24-hour flight required pilots to be alert with their thought processes intact and in a safe mode for proper handling of weaponry. It was believed that using modafinil did not cause any agitation. We have learned quite a bit about this drug since then.

Modafinil goes straight to the wake up center of the brain and is commonly used for narcolepsy. It gives people a wide-awake, alert feeling, allowing them to function without feelings of drowsiness. It does this by increasing the stimulant effects of glutamate and noradrenaline in the brain, while decreasing the GABA. Taking modafinil also has a pleasurable side effect because it increases the nucleus accumbens' release of dopamine. While this drug does have its place in treatment protocol, using it daily can eventually lead to a neurotransmitter imbalance, as in the case of this woman.

Detoxification off Modafinil: This is a very complicated case with lots of neurotransmitter systems involved. This patient has tried to taper off the drug dosage in the past and failed. Simply stopping the drug will lead to further complications in this detoxification; therefore we need a methodology to figure out how to get this patient off modafinil for good. We need to think in terms of neurotransmitter balances. When using this methodology, we must consider how the neurotransmitters are affected and the results of these effects.

Modafinil raises glutamate, which makes the brain aware and alert and is toxic at high levels. It increases noradrenaline, also resulting in awareness. It increases dopamine, causing pleasure. It suppresses GABA, the neurotransmitter that has a sedating effect, slowing the brain. The over-all effect is increased activity in the brain with minimal agitation and cardiovascular repercussions. While attempting to counteract modafinil's

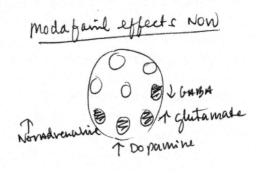

inhibitory effect on GABA, she also became addicted to lorazepam (Ativan), a benzodiazepine drug that hits GABA1a receptor sites and is primarily used in the management of acute anxiety and insomnia. In addition, her dopamine production is being further stimulated with the Abilify she is using.

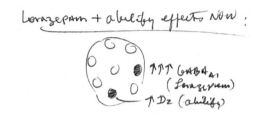

To summarize this analysis, I find it helpful to first write down all the neurochemical effects of modafinil on one side of the page: increased glutamate, decreased GABA, increased noradrenaline, and increased dopamine. Also note that due to the Ativan (lorazepam) she is on, her GABA is increased. Then on the other side of the page, jot down what will happen to these neurotransmitters once the modafinil and lorazepam are discontinued: glutamate will drop, noradrenaline will drop, dopamine will drop, and GABA

will likely decrease because of the halted lorazepam. These changes will lead to hypersomnolence.

Now we must make sure the detoxification goes as safely and smoothly as possible. After finding the source of her symptoms and discontinuing the drugs, the next step is to stimulate the GABA system, but this time <u>without</u> hitting the GABA1a site. To do this, we will use phenobarbital, Robaxin, and possibly Neurontin. We will increase her noradrenaline with Cymbalta (which actually raises both noradrenaline and serotonin). Her dopamine could be increased with either bupropion or Abilify. We will artificially raise these neurotransmitters, but allow the patient's inherent glutamate to slowly increase on its own. When we take this approach, we are maintaining easy arousability in the patient and making sure that the patient's fatigue does not interfere with her cardiovascular or respiratory response.

This patient's detoxification was a success. With proper analysis of the drug-induced neurochemical abnormalities and use of the methods just discussed, we have a theoretical guide to direct us through the detoxification. Using this methodology in our approach allows us to know which neurotransmitters to adjust and then use the appropriate medications to combat the state of detoxification.

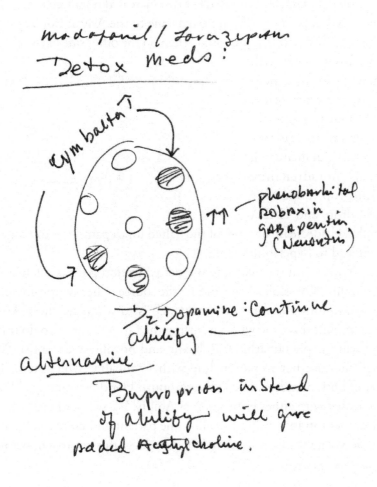

Case Study #2
Anticipating Neurotransmitter Reactions

Patient Profile: A 76-year-old artery bypass graft patient with chronic obstructive pulmonary disease and alcoholism has had a complicated course of treatment. He was given Dilaudid (an opiate) as well as significant amounts of Ativan. The patient was very sensitive to these medications, and he became drastically obtunded.

The nurse is asking what she should do.

Neurotransmitter Analysis: We must first look at what caused the obtundation. It was a result of the two above-mentioned drugs. Ativan caused a significant GABA effect at the GABA1a sites, and the administered Dilaudid drove up the opiate center. The end result of this opiate and GABA stimulation was

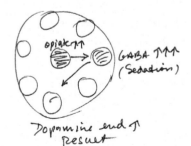

a dopamine effect. To reduce the effects of these drugs, we must now use what we call *competitive inhibitors* to act as blockers for those sites.

If we administer naltrexone or Narcan, these molecules will competitively hover around the opiate sites, competing with the Dilaudid so that it can no longer stimulate the opiate receptor sites. Then the opiates would not be able to affect the nucleus accumbens and other areas of the brain and spinal cord. This method could wake up the patient. The other option, Romazicon, would hover around the multiple GABA sites throughout the brain. If administered, Romazicon would act as a competitive inhibitor for the Ativan or benzodiazepine that is currently hitting the GABA1a sites and slowing the patient down so much that he is obtunded. It would basically disable the Ativan from working and possibly cause the patient to wake up.

The question now is whether to use Narcan or Romazicon. Using Narcan would likely be successful in waking up the patient. Using the Romazicon would suddenly block all GABA receptors, and in doing so could not only wake up the patient, but also possibly cause him to become severely agitated, even to the point of having a grand mal seizure. Due to this risk of seizure activity and the fact that complete inhibition of the GABA system would likely cause further agitation for an alcoholic in withdrawal, we decided to hold off on the Romazicon and give the patient Narcan instead.

Lesson: It is important to make a practice out of visualizing receptor sites and to understand the various neurotransmitter systems. For example, the opiate and GABA systems are very closely tied and work together

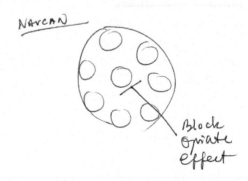

to cause the obtundation and/or depression of the patient. Being aware of these kinds of facts gives a physician clear treatment options to choose from, rather than just making an intuitive choice. In this kind of case, a physician must consider the two systems being most affected that are connected to each other and the receptor sites that can be subject to competitive inhibitory action. That requires a deeper knowledge than just making a random choice, which could lead to an unwanted outcome.

Case Study #3
OxyContin Abuse

Patient Profile: An 18-year-old female with a history of alcoholism now snorts high doses of OxyContin. In the past, she was a blackout drinker who began drinking alcohol excessively at the age of fifteen. Her drinking landed her in the emergency room twice for alcohol overdose. Though she has no chronic pain syndrome, her addiction to opiates began two years ago with Vicodin and she quickly switched to OxyContin. In addition to her drug and alcohol problems, she suffers from some post-traumatic stress disorder, having been the victim of rape on two different occasions, one of which was associated with alcohol. Though she is adopted,

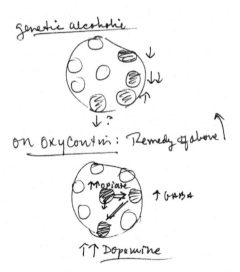

her biological father was also an alcoholic. It appears she is a genetic alcoholic using opiates to remedy her inherited neurotransmitter imbalances.

Detoxification off OxyContin: Once her detoxification starts, her serotonin, GABA, opiate, and dopamine levels will all decrease rapidly. The best way to handle this and detoxify her off these opiates safely is through the GABA system. Many physicians still use the front door approach, slowly tapering them off alternative opiates like Suboxone, but the insurance company wants this patient detoxified in five days or less. In this back door method, we will use the stimulation of her GABA receptor sites to help her opiate system up-regulate. GABA drugs in fact stimulate the opiate system and vice versa. Phenobarbital, Neurontin (a glutamate inhibitor), Robaxin (a GABA-like drug), and baclofen (a GABA drug) will all be utilized in a nontoxic manner. This method of detoxification is fast, relatively painless, and very successful.

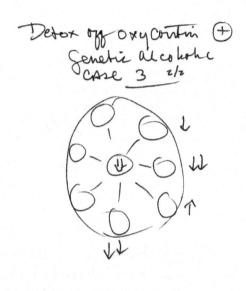

Beyond the Detoxification – Treating Cravings to Avoid Relapse: When detoxifying this patient off OxyContin, we also need to take into consideration the possibility that she might be a cross-addicted genetic alcoholic. Therefore once she is detoxified, a neurochemical imbalance due to her genetics will in all probability still remain. This could mean future cravings and relapse. Cravings that result from inherited neurotransmitter imbalances and are sparked by typical cues of daily life need to be addressed. Selective serotonin re-uptake inhibitors (SSRI) that increase serotonin and medications that adjust the GABA-glutamate balance (like Campral and Topamax) can be useful in benefiting such problematic imbalances. Remember, alcohol stimulates serotonin 5HT3, GABA, and dopamine. Opiates hit GABA and then dopamine. The end result is much the same, thus the cross-addiction.

Looking at her history of alcohol consumption, she was likely chasing after the euphoric effects of the beta endorphin release and dopamine surge that occur in the nucleus accumbens. Maintaining that state of euphoria is difficult to do and as in her case, often leads to blackout and overdose. Her switch from alcohol abuse to opiate abuse is not surprising. OxyContin has been providing her with that same euphoric dopamine effect without the risk of blacking out. However, she could now overdose and die.

The best course for us now will be to detoxify her as planned and observe her closely for indications of any other mood disorders. Additionally, using naltrexone to block the opiate system and dopamine release would also be beneficial, allowing the dopamine receptors to up-regulate. Naltrexone or the injectable form of it, called Vivitrol, may also block the nucleus accumbens so that the high-dose effect of any opiates that she tries to use in the near future will be blocked. Vivitrol and naltrexone can also block the high-dose opiate release that alcohol causes. Since this patient is so young, we are going to place her in a 28-day program where she will either receive naltrexone daily or be given Vivitrol which lasts for one month. The end result will be a decrease in her craving for alcohol and the blocking of opiate receptor sites. Naltrexone acts as a competitive inhibitor, so if a person takes a narcotic, such as OxyContin, the person will neither get sick, nor get a high. This is the beauty of keeping someone on naltrexone after ten days of detoxification.

Remember: It is important to use the method of neurotransmitter evaluation and analysis to not only detoxify patients off currently abused drugs, but also to resolve any underlying genetic neurochemical deficiencies, thereby averting future cravings and relapse.

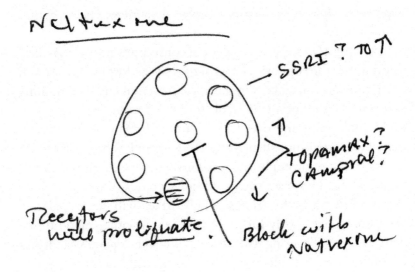

Naltrexone

SSRI? to ↑

Topamax?
Campral?

Receptors
will proliferate.

Block with
Naltrexone

Case Study #4
Benzodiazepine and Opiate Detoxification of a Self-Medicating Bipolar Patient

Patient Profile: A 38-year-old San Franciscan barista was diagnosed with bipolar disorder and placed on Lamictal but still suffers from racing thoughts and anxiety. The patient tries to control his racing thoughts by taking both #14 Norco and 8mg of Xanax a day, along with the 175 mg of the prescribed Lamictal. This patient can no longer control the rapid thoughts and is feeling helpless to the increasing amounts of drugs he is taking. With his anxiety out of control, neither the Xanax, nor the Norco is effective in easing his feelings of hopelessness.

He has been on methadone in the past and used cocaine extensively while in college. He is the married father of a 17-month-old daughter, and the son of an alcoholic.

Analysis: By taking Norco, this patient is using the opiate system to try to control the racing thoughts and undesirable mania associated with bipolar disorder. The opiate center definitely has a strong tie to GABA and the dopamine center (where most bipolar people often have some sort of imbalance), and that is why many bipolar patients self-medicate with opiates to try to slow themselves down. Since his father was an alcoholic, this patient may be using the opiate system not only to stimulate the dopamine system, but possibly

Case Study 4

Norco Xanax & lamictal

Norco's = Opiate → GABA → Dopamine
Lamictal has some GABA effect.

other deficient neurotransmitter systems as well. Judging by his past and present choices in drugs, he is likely driving the opiate system to talk to both his dopamine and GABA systems.

Aside from opiates, he is also abusing Xanax, a benzodiazepine GABA1a site activating drug, in high doses to try to calm himself down and control his mania. So in all, he is currently using large amounts of Xanax, Norco, and the GABA drug Lamictal, all in attempt to slow himself down. In the past he tried to do this with methadone.

Detoxification: To detoxify this patient, we will use heavy GABA stimulation of four of the five GABA sites, leaving the GABA1a site (where the Xanax has been hitting) untouched. We arrive at our choices for medications by looking at the drugs he is already using, thus determining the deficiencies he is trying to account for. Clearly he is trying to combat rapid activity in his brain by using the opiate and GABA systems. There is a safer and more effective way to ease his anxiety and racing thoughts, and that is by means of the GABA system (minus use of the unpredictable GABA1a site). Using other GABA sites, such as those activated by phenobarbital, Neurontin (a glutamate inhibitor), and other atypical and antiseizure medications in the GABA family, will result in a safe detoxification and get his racing thoughts under control.

Discontinuing the Xanax and not using any Valium or diaze-pam-like drugs will mean a significant drop in his opiates, dopa-mine, and GABA as his body goes into detoxification, but this will allow the GABA1a sites to up-regulate. Meanwhile, we will continue to inhibit the glutamate with Neurontin and utilize the other GABA sites with the Lamictal, along with short-acting nontoxic high-doses of phenobarbital. We will control his anxiety with another GABA-like drug, baclofen. If the patient ends up

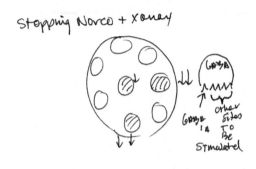

Stopping Norco + Xanay

GABA

other sites

GABA 1a to be stimulated

having some episodic mania, it is best to use a bipolar-appropriate drug. These GABA-like drugs will talk to the opiate system, allowing him to successfully detoxify off both the heavy narcotics and the benzodiazepines in a quick and safe manner. He will be detoxified in four days.

Afterthoughts: This patient did quite well after the detoxifica-tion, experiencing less anxiety and fewer racing thoughts. The racing thoughts were a result of the severe imbalance between his GABA and glutamate. Essentially, there were not enough GABA brakes to counteract his glutamate gas pedal. His GABA1a receptor sites had become so severely down-regulated with the medications he was taking, that his high glutamate was left virtually unopposed. This is an example of the paradoxical effect that occurs when the GABA1a sites get so over-loaded that suddenly these sites that are supposed to put on the brakes of the brain activity, no longer have any brake pads. With the proper treatment as demonstrated above, where all GABA1a stimulating drugs are stopped, the brain will find its balance and the GABA will repair itself. The patient will become calmer with the brain-in-balance phenomenon.

Case Study #5
Benzodiazepine Withdrawal

Patient Profile: A 73-year-old opiate-dependent patient enters the ICU after undergoing coronary artery bypass surgery. He is currently taking 30mg of methadone per day, 5mg of Valium three times a day, and 4 to 5mg of morphine sulfate every hour. His condition stabilizes, so he is moved to the ward.

In the ward, his progress takes an unexpected turn. His blood pressure reaches 170/110 with a pulse of 112. He becomes diaphoretic and experiences an increased amount of confusion. His pulse oximeter reads 98 percent with an unchanged electrocardiodiagram. The patient is moaning.

Diagnosis: A review of the patient's medications revealed that he is no longer taking any GABA benzodiazepines, neither Ativan, nor Valium. Moreover,

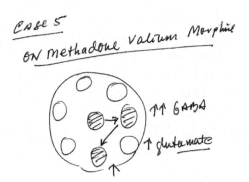

CASE 5

ON methadone Valium Morphine

↑↑ GABA

↑ glutamate

he is now receiving two narcotic pain relievers, a fentanyl patch at 25 µg and 4mg of Dilaudid every three hours. The symptoms this patient is suffering from are caused by the GABA1a site not being stimulated in the past 24 hours, leading to an unopposed glutamate effect and acute GABA1a detoxification (a.k.a. benzodiazepine withdrawal).

Misreading the symptoms, the house physician ordered more fentanyl intravenously, thinking that the patient was having severe pain syndrome. Another physician ordered Haldol, a D2 dopamine inhibitor. The problem with these medications is they are not addressing the real issue. Add-

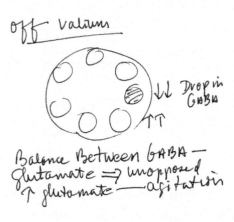

ing more opiates will do little to help his GABA1a site deficiency, though the two systems are connected. As mentioned earlier, the patient has not received the GABA1a site agonistic effects of benzodiazepines for the past 24 hours. The obvious diagnosis is benzodiazepine withdrawal. This unopposed GABA deficiency along with increased chance of seizure activity brought on by Haldol, could lead to a seizure.

Afterward: This patient received 1mg of Ativan intravenously and immediately his pulse decreased, and the patient was far less agitated. Thereafter, 5mg of Valium was prescribed three times a day on a regular basis to prevent further benzodiazepine withdrawal. The patient was also placed on 200mg of Tegretol put orally twice a day for its GABA effect on other GABA receptor sites, in order to prevent seizure activity. The fentanyl and Haldol were discontinued.

Case Study #6
An Opiate and Alcohol Detoxification

Patient Profile: A 32-year-old female with a family history of alcoholism had been seeing her addictionologist for opiate dependency and was being treated with 25mg of Suboxone per day. She had been attending a group on a regular basis, where she was identified as having a mood disorder as well as some depression. The patient was previously on Norco and Vicodin and had switched over to Suboxone for continued detoxification, but she did not detoxify well and has been on Suboxone for the last three months. Approximately two weeks prior to my meeting her, her physician had decreased her dosage of Suboxone due to her small physical size.

Suboxone is a combination of the narcotic buprenorphine and naltrexone (an opiate blocker commonly used to treat opiate addiction). Being in relative withdrawal with an increased amount of tolerance, when her physician decreased the Suboxone, she started drinking high-doses of alcohol while still taking the prescribed medication. Suboxone had been stimulating the opiate system and when the dosage was decreased, suddenly her genetic alcoholism and craving for alcohol surfaced. The patient became severely intoxicated. 9-1-1 was contacted, and she was taken to the emergency room.

The Suboxone failed. She now needs to be detoxified off of both alcohol and Suboxone. There are several challenges in this situation. Not only must we detoxify the patient off opiates, but we must

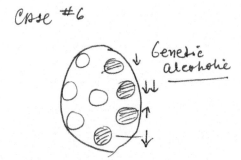

Case #6

↓ Genetic alcoholic

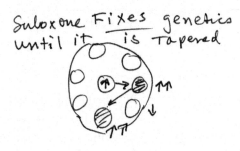

Suboxone Fixes genetics until it is Tapered

also treat the cravings linked to genetic alcoholism.

Detoxification and Prevention: Rather than continuing to direct treatment towards hitting opiate receptors by using opiate drugs, we will use an entirely different approach. To get this patient off opiates, we will use the back door method, where we stop the narcotics and stimulate receptor sites of the GABA system. We will use phenobarbital, Neurontin, Robaxin, Tegretol, Topamax, and baclofen – all GABA or GABA-like drugs. Thanks to the central opiate system and its strong connection the GABA system, these GABA drugs will be used to bring our patient in for a smooth landing off of Suboxone.

To treat the cravings for alcohol, we will focus our treatment on three of the five neurotransmitter systems alcohol readily affects – serotonin, GABA, and glutamate. We know that genetic alcoholics often are low in serotonin, so for now we will put her on Lexapro, a selective serotonin re-uptake inhibitor (SSRI). (Other serotonins could be used – remember you are playing with approximately 22 subtypes of 5HTs or serotonins) We will also put her on Campral and Topamax, which both target and help restore GABA-like effects. This in turn positively affects dopamine and brings the glutamate and GABA systems into a healthy balance with each other.

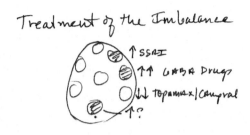

Treatment of the Imbalance

↑ SSRI
↑↑ GABA Drug
↓↓ Topamax / Campral
↑ ?

This patient had a good detoxification. She went back to her primary care physician on the above-mentioned medications (with the exception of any phenobarbital, since that drug can be addictive).

Unexpected Complications: Five hours after the patient is discharged, she suddenly arrives at the detoxification unit again, this time diaphoretic and tremulous. With very sweaty palms, she has intense feelings of dysphoria. Her blood pressure is 160/110 with a pulse of 90. The admitting nurse thinks that this is continued detoxification.

But what really happened here? More precisely, what happened on a neurochemical basis? Were these new symptoms a part of continued detoxification off of high-dose Suboxone and alcohol? Would the patient need to be placed in a chemical dependency unit and be given Suboxone and/or phenobarbital?

The Missing Clue: Her primary care physician thought it would be beneficial to add an antidepressant drug to the mix, and prescribed Effexor, thinking only that it was a dopaminergic drug. Unbeknownst to him, Effexor also has noradrenaline. Experiencing effects similar to that of taking adrenaline, within half an hour of taking the Effexor, the patient said, "I felt weird." She developed hypertension and tachycardia.

Now What To Do: We added a beta-blocker, which slowed down her heart rate and decreased her blood pressure. The patient felt much better, drinking lots of fluids and essentially metabolizing the Effexor over 24 hours. Don't get me wrong – Effexor is a great drug for depression because of its noradrenergic and serotonin effects. However, I believe it was too much noradrenaline for this patient's case. It can get very complex when you are trying to figure out what is going on. But let me tell you, if it weren't for these techniques I am teaching you in this book, I would be lost and I think you would be too. I am not one who likes to guess at these things.

How did we know this was not just a continuation of the detoxification process – a sudden and unexpected rapid acceleration of detoxification from Suboxone and alcohol?

Review: There exists a maximal amount of down-regulation. Regardless of the amount of drugs taken, detoxifications always follow a timetable (the one laid out in the detoxification curve) that we in the field of detoxification are very familiar with. The degree of withdrawal symptoms is not dependent upon how much narcotics a patient takes. Just because this patient was on a high dosage of Suboxone and alcohol, does not mean that she was going to have a more intense or longer detoxification than someone coming off just a couple grams of heroin or even #60 Norco a day. That is because there exists a maximum amount of suppression of the opiate receptor sites. The degree or intensity of detoxification symptoms come from down-regulation or changes that have been made to these sites, by varying amounts of opiates. Withdrawal symptoms are felt as the receptor sites are trying to come back to a normal state once they are not longer stimulated by high dose narcotics.

I am trying to think of a way to convince you of the fact that once someone exceeds a certain amount of damage to their receptor sites, there is a ceiling that is reached where the detoxification will not get any worse, no matter how much of a drug a patient has been using. I cannot tell you how many times doctors and addictionologists have said that they cannot detoxify someone because they are taking huge amounts of opiates. For example, I have heard the following scenarios over the phone: 400 mg of methadone a day, 400 µg of fentanyl an hour, 4 grams heroin a day, twenty to thirty 80 mg of OxyContin a day, and 100 pills of combinations of these drugs per day. When I hear those numbers on the phone, along with a request to detoxify these patients in four days, I think of how suppressed or how much these patients' neuroreceptors are out of balance. "*Maximally*," I reason. The amount of drug becomes superfluous when thinking that one has to detoxify or get the brain in balance. What I have gained in resolving thousands of these scary huge pill-takers' cases, is the appreciation that there is a ceiling where the brain can only change so much when it is hammered by huge amounts of drugs.

It is also important to note that the combining of high-dose opiates with alcohol does not create a magnified degree of detoxification. Often the detoxification will liken either the symptoms of an opiate detoxification or an alcohol detoxification, but not a combination of the two.

Another important situation to consider, which further illustrates this concept, is when patients go through rapid detoxification. In this case naltrexone or a competitive inhibitor hovers around the opiate sites and the patient goes into acute withdrawal. Once these receptor sites are blocked, you will see the maximum amount of detoxification of the patient. In other words, it does not matter how many molecules of opiates there are hitting the receptor sites, because there are a limited number of sites, depending on the individual, that are available to be activated. This ultimately means that there is a limit to both the amount of down-regulation and up-regulation possible.

The Final Rule: As a physician, you are not detoxifying the amount of narcotic, benzodiazepine, alcohol, or any other drug; you are detoxifying the damage or the changes that have been made to those receptor sites in the brain.

Case Study #7
Bipolar Patient Addicted to Opiates

Patient Profile: A 42-year-old auto worker takes 6mg of Xanax and #12 Norco every day. He has a long history of both drug use and bipolar disorder. Alcoholism also runs in the family. Not too long ago, he was detoxified off of 100mg of methadone a day, using a rapid detoxification method. Since then, he has been on 150mg of Lamictal a day and Lexapro on a regular basis.

He now wants a five day detoxification to stop the Xanax and Norco and to get his bipolar disorder and racing thoughts under control. Otherwise, his physical examination is normal.

Drug Effects: By using Xanax at 6mg a day, this patient is putting his GABA1a site in hyperdrive. The high dosage of Norco he uses is stimulating the central opiate system, thus stimulating the other seven systems, since they are all connected. To complicate matters, there is a close association between benzodiazepine-driven GABA1a sites and the

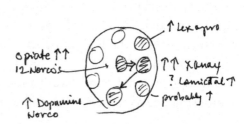

opiate system, so they play off each other, driving one another even further.

Looking at the Eight Systems: Most likely, this patient has a dopaminergic deficiency and possibly even a noradrenergic problem related to his bipolar disorder. The genetic alcoholism he inherited from his father means that he could have a deficiency in either one or more of the following neurotransmitter systems: serotonin, glutamate, GABA, endocannabinoid, and opiate. It is common for genetic alcoholics to become cross-addicted to opiates rather than alcohol, because the central opiate system will compensate for various genetic deficiencies.

Remember, roughly 50 percent of the reason that most people use drugs and alcohol is due to inherited problems in their genetic hardware. This man's genetic inheritance of both alcoholism and

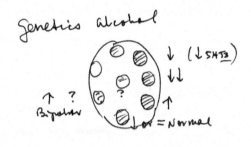

bipolar disorder make him a prime candidate for opiate addiction. This makes stabilizing him while removing the Norco and benzodiazepines quite a challenge. We will need to follow the schematic of the neurotransmitter systems to ensure success.

Treatment: A multi-faceted case like this is a challenge, yet we deal with this kind on a weekly basis. Analyzing what is happening on a neurochemical level is the first step. Then we will stop the Xanax so that the GABA1a site will have no activation. This would make the patient go into GABA withdrawal and ultimately a seizure if left unchecked. To avoid this, we will stimulate the other GABA sites to counteract the high glutamate. We will also immediately stop the Norco. With the opiate system left bare, the patient will go into opiate withdrawal. Recall though, that there is a strong relationship between the GABA and opiate systems; they are the married couple. Therefore by strongly stimulating the other four GABA sites, not only are we compensating for the lack of GABA1a stimulation, but also the new absence of opiates.

The patient is already taking GABA-like Lamictal, which is stimulating the third or fourth GABA sites. We are going to drive the GABA higher by administering nontoxic doses of phenobarbital. Every hour, 30 to 60mg of phenobarbital will be administered and serum monitored daily to make sure the patient is not toxic. Over the course of three to four days, we can raise the Lamictal and add Seroquel, a D2 dopamine and 5-HT2 serotonin antagonist, several times a day to treat the bipolar disorder. We might also add a dopaminergic effect by giving a D2 drug such as Abilify.

There are many ways to approach treatment, depending on the patient's current neurochemical abnormality. If Abilify, a dopamine agonist, is added and the patient already has too much D2, it could

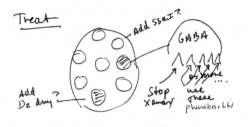

lead to more agitation and hallucinosis. Caution must be used when devising a treatment plan for these complicated cases. No matter what method is used, there are always flaws in everything we do. We just strive to be within critical standard deviations.

The Results: We ended up giving this patient 5mg of dopamine in the morning and 200mg of Seroquel at nighttime. We stopped the phenobarbital in five days. His condition had vastly improved; he was calm, collected, and focused.

Highlights to Remember: (1) Bipolar patients love opiates because they drive all other systems, especially the dopamine system. (2) The GABA and opiate systems are closely tied. (3) By stimulating the other four GABA sites, leaving the GABA1a site without activation, we can successfully modulate the opiate center. (4) Most of the time, dopamine seems to work well in getting mania and bipolar disorder under control.

Case Study #8
A Genetic Alcoholic on Opiates

Patient Profile: A 55-year-old female genetic alcoholic has been hospitalized multiple times for major depressive episodes. She has attended several programs in the past and has many immediate family members who are also alcoholics. She has a history of using high-dose Norco at #15 to #20 a day, in addition to morphine sulfate.

Under the qualified care of an addictionologist, she has been taking Suboxone up to 20mg a day, helping her to quit both drinking and using opiates. She continued on Lexapro, Wellbutrin, and 300mg of Seroquel at night. However, over the course of 1 ½ years, the dosage of Suboxone was cut in half, and the patient suddenly started drinking heavily again. Drinking one to two bottles of wine per day, she blacked out on a regular basis and started taking more Ativan (a benzodiazepine).

She was rushed to the emergency room for overdose. It seems that once the opiate center had fewer stimuli from Suboxone, she had a relapse on alcoholism. This is a very common scenario: Opiates are being tapered and everything is going fine until suddenly the opiates are dropped to a level where the patient's craving for alcohol kicks in and *bam!!!* You now have a relapse. That is when you know you have a genetic alcoholic on your hands.

Analysis and Treatment Course: The patient is placed in our detoxification unit. She is an infamous blackout drinker, meaning she uses high-dose alcohol to the point of having her nucleus accumbens release its own opium beta-endorphin, which in turn leads to the release of dopamine. These kinds of drinkers chase the dopamine high until they blackout. While she was on a high enough dose of Suboxone, the patient's craving for alcohol and need for further opiates were fulfilled.

The first step in her treatment is to stop all narcotics and alcohol. We also stopped the Ativan immediately. We now have before us (1) a bare opiate system that without further stimulus, is currently going into opiate withdrawal and (2) a GABA center with an over-worked and destroyed GABA1a site because of damage from the Ativan. On top of that, she has significant depression. Due to the increased seizure risk that comes with the detoxification, the bare opiate system, and the stopped Ativan, we discontinued the Wellbutrin (because of *its* possible seizure risk). We will continue to give her Seroquel during the daytime.

The opiate system will up-regulate significantly once in detoxification. We must remember that since she is a genetic alcoholic, her cravings could be the result of deficiencies and imbalances in a number of different neurotransmitter systems – glutamate, GABA, endocannabi-

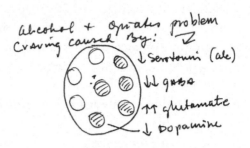

noid, serotonin, opiate, or possibly even dopamine. Remember, alcohol affects a vast number of neurotransmitters.

Since the GABA and opiate system are closely tied, we will use heavy GABA to detoxify the patient. But because of the damage done to the GABA1a site, we will not be using any benzo-diazepines. We will give her baclofen, which is a GABA drug, and will place her on high-dose Neurontin, Tegretol, and phenobarbital in nontoxic doses to prevent seizure activity. Since she is a genetic

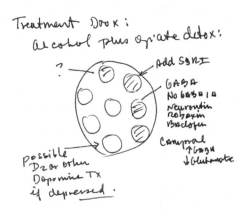

alcoholic, we will make sure that she has stimulus to the serotonin system by giving her Lexapro, a selective serotonin re-uptake inhibitor (SSRI). We will also give her Campral to balance out and help the GABA - glutamate balance.

Fast Results: The patient was detoxified in four days, and did not have any further cravings. Dopamine (that is, Abilify) was used as a D2 drug to support the patient's dopaminergic system since opiates and alcohol were no longer stimulating the dopamine system as they once were. We found this necessary due to the fact that she used to be addicted to methamphetamine, an illicit drug with some dopaminergic effect. The patient did well with this combination and was discharged from the detoxification unit on Lexapro, 400mg of Neurontin four times a day, 10mg of baclofen three times a day, 300mg of Seroquel at night, and 666mg of Campral three times a day.

It is Important to Remember: Genetic alcoholics commonly use the opiate system to satisfy the needs of the alcohol system (the six neurotransmitter systems affected by alcohol) because the end results of both high-dose alcohol and high-dose opiates is to achieve a euphoric dopamine effect. Once the opiate system stimulus is decreased to a certain point, the alcohol system suddenly emerges with cravings and ultimately a relapse. Therefore, administering an opiate like Suboxone and then tapering it off, does not typically work to solve opiate/alcohol cross addiction if the underlying problem is a genetic alcoholic neurotransmitter imbalance. That is why there are so many relapses throughout the country among patients who complete rehab programs with detoxification. Without genetic neurotransmitter deficiency analysis, risk of relapse significantly increases due to craving – the sign of a neurochemical imbalance.

Case Study #9
Common Complications in the ICU

Patient Profile: A 67-year old professional came in to the ICU with a cardiac arrest and then had a balloon pump and a five-vessel coronary artery bypass graft. He required intubation. In the past, this patient had been using benzodiazepines in small doses, and liked to drink four shots of alcohol per night. His family also informed me that he had been in the Vietnam War and suffered from some post-traumatic stress disorder (PTSD).

ICU Care Thus Far: An earlier attempt to extubate the patient lead to marked anxiety, disorientation, and hyperventilation, causing progressive hypoxemia with the patient's ejection fraction in the 40 percent range. The patient needed to be reintubated and was then placed on propofol, narcotics, and a high-dose Versed intravenous continuous drip. Each time they discontinued the propofol, the patient would hyperventilate and decompensate, and propofol would have to be immediately administered again. A chest x-ray revealed an infiltrate, and the patient was on 30 percent oxygen on the ventilator.

The Plan: First and foremost, we must discontinue all narcotics and benzodiazepines, meaning all opiates and GABA1a drugs. Then we must place the patient on Diprivan (propofol) for only two or three days. The lorazepam GABA1a drug with its fifteen-hour half-life will metabolize within two days. Versed, with its even shorter half-life will also be discontinued. With the patient on standard cardiac drugs and continuing on the ventilator oxygenating at 100 percent, there are no signs of cerebrovascular accident, nor any other neurological pathology. After the first 24 hours, 25mg of Seroquel will be placed in the nasogastric tube three times a day.

The Outcome: Once the propofol was discontinued the next day, phenobarbital (a sedating GABA drug) was administered in 30mg doses every hour. We made sure the phenobarbital was kept at nontoxic levels by monitoring it in laboratory evaluation. This patient awoke after three days, uncomplicated and was extubated within four hours after he had good blood gases. Taking into consideration his history of post-traumatic stress disorder, we controlled his anxiety with the Seroquel. Had we not changed the drugs administered to this patient, he likely would have continued on the ventilator for much longer, with the pulmonary status only worsening and costs for medical care increasing.

Review: The GABA1a sites were likely down-regulated and desensitized due to previous benzodiazepine (valium) use. This lack of active GABA1a sites and increase in unopposed glutamate added to his anxiety. The lorazepam needed to be stopped before any further down-regulation of the GABA1a sites occurred. This allowed the GABA sites to regain functionality and thereby decreased the patient's anxiety within the next few weeks. The PTSD, which is essentially emotional trauma leading to significant neurotransmitter and other imbalances, is believed to be associated with a noradrenergic surging of the brain's Amygdala. Seroquel and/or prazosin act to quell this surging. The blood pressure medicine prazosin is an alpha adrenergic blocker.

Case Study #10
Off the Ventilator and Extubated

Patient Profile: A 65-year-old professional was admitted to the ICU after having two cardiac arrests with a balloon pump, a cardiac bypass, and a valve replacement. He has been in the ICU, intubated and on a ventilator for seven days now. He has suffered from a significant amount of anxiety in the past, and has a history of taking Xanax in the morning. He also has obsessive-compulsive traits. His family tells me that he is not an alcoholic, but that he does enjoy drinking two beers every night.

His Initial ICU Experience: Every time the medical staff decreases this man's propofol dosage, the patient becomes severely agitated and tries to pull out his lines and his tube. On one occasion he sat up and looking with a blank stare, began to hyperventilate and went into acute and aggravated hypoxemia and had to be reintubated. The medical staff has him on cardiac drugs and high doses of lorazepam, a benzodiazepine. Each time he wakes up, he is confused and agitated and has a panic attack. It is possible that the lorazepam that he is receiving intravenously is causing this agitation, through a paradoxical effect at the GABA1a site.

How to Treat this Patient's Neurochemical Abnormalities: We will continue to maintain this patient's sedation with the propofol. Since the patient was on the ventilator and under the sedation of propofol, the best thing to do is stop the GABA1a site paradoxical effect by halting the lorazepam. Lorazepam has a fifteen-hour half-life and will be mostly metabolized in three days. Therefore, if we stop the lorazepam, the other sedative hypnotics, and the narcotics together on day one and keep him on the propofol or Precedex for an additional two or three days, he will awake and come off the ventilator nicely when we discontinue the propofol or Precedex. Starting 24 hours before he begins to awake, we will give him 25mg of Seroquel three times a day. We will treat his anxiety by administering 30 mg of phenobarbital (a GABA drug that does not hit the GABA1a site) intravenously every thirty minutes as needed.

Results: This patient awoke, opened his eyes, looked at his surroundings, and was bereft of any agitation and tremulousness. A small dose of phenobarbital was given once again after the patient started awakening more, and soon he was extubated successfully.

Lessons: (1) Investigating prior psychological diagnoses such as general anxiety disorder and panic attacks was a significant part of treating this patient's anxiety successfully. (2) Considering the benzodiazepine as a paradoxical effect drug and knowing the neurotransmitter systems well enough to know whether this is a possibility or not were necessary tools to this patient's successful extubation. A multifactorial approach based on psychological evidence and neurotransmitter status lead to success in this very difficult intensive care addiction medicine case.

Case Study #11
Acute Opiate Withdrawal in the Hospital

Patient Profile: A 73-year-old male has had a six week stay in the hospital after having a femoral-popliteal bypass. He had suffered from painful ischemia and a clot in his leg. Fortunately his leg was saved with a revision of the femoral-popliteal bypass and debridement of the ischemia. He is now ready to be discharged.

While in the hospital, he has received Ativan, Dilaudid, morphine, and other high dose narcotics. His pain is 90 percent better; however, since he has refused to take any more narcotics in the past 24 hours, he is suffering from acute withdrawal. He is diaphoretic and nauseated with muscle cramps and aching all over. He also has restless legs and cannot sleep at night. His family wants to know what to do.

Medications and Mechanisms to Consider: We know that in acute opiate withdrawal, one's glutamate and noradrenaline are at increased levels. Taking this into consideration, we will increase

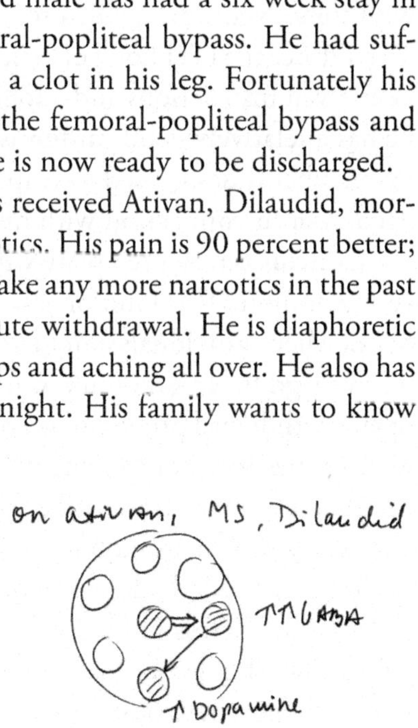

on ativan, MS, Dilaudid

↑↑ GABA

↑ Dopamine

his dosage of gabapentin to 400mg four times a day. We also need the effects of GABA to decrease his muscular pain (myalgia), so he will be given 500mg of Robaxin four times a day. If these GABA drugs do not already get his restless leg syndrome under control, we will use Requip (a dopamine

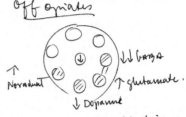

type of drug) to do the trick. We will also give him phenobarbital in titrating doses with a peak at approximately the third day.

The patient did not want to take any Suboxone or any other narcotics because he *just wants off.* His sleep will be controlled with amitriptyline, an antidepressant drug that he has been on in the past. He has some peripheral damage, so the amitriptyline, along with some Neurontin, will also help control his neuropathic pain. To reinforce the likelihood of a successful detoxification, at discharge he is given instructions and a follow-up appointment. Fortunately he has a relatively good cardiovascular system. In addition, a family member is designated to help him through any issues he might encounter in connection with his treatment.

Conclusion: Acute opiate withdrawal in the hospital setting is very common. This kind of case is typical throughout the United States when individuals enter the hospital for some procedure and receive significant amounts of narcotics. They are often left with opiate withdrawal problems, even after their pain issues are resolved with proper medical treatment. It most frequently occurs among patients who have back surgeries or orthopedic procedures. This also seems to be common among men over sixty who suffer from cardiac events. Methadone and Suboxone are commonly prescribed medications in this kind of case, and they do work well if titrated effectively. This man's case is typical for a patient who does not want any more narcotics.

This patient did very well on an outpatient basis with his detoxification. By using medications, we successfully alleviated some of the withdrawal symptoms in connection with detoxification. Ultimately we got him off of the medications that were causing him dysphoria and other side effects, and helped restore his brain to its natural balance as painlessly as possible. He required further treatment on a chemical basis after his hospitalization. I hear that his cardiovascular status has stabilized.

Case Study #12
Xanax and a GABA Deficiency

Patient Profile: A 73-year-old college professor made the mistake of drinking while taking his anxiety medication, Xanax. He was charged with a DUI. His medical history includes a coronary bypass graft, tachycardia, and panic attacks. He has been taking Xanax for several years now. He and his doctor want him to be detoxified. The patient recently tried cutting back on his high-dose Xanax, taking only one half of a milligram every two hours. The result was a near-seizure experience along with violent emesis, insomnia, shaking, and tremulousness.

The Source of the Problem: This is clearly a GABA problem. Patients with anxiety issues typically get placed on medications that stimulate their GABA production at the GABA1a site. As you recall, this can be a very unpredictable site once it has been overused. It is not uncommon for patients to experience a paradoxical effect from continual over-stimulation of this site.

That is what has occurred here with this patient. Basically, he naturally has very low GABA and what GABA stimulation he does have, has virtually all been driven by hitting the GABA1a site with Xanax. The GABA1a site is essentially "worn out" and he has high tolerance at that location. Once he started to take the Xanax away, he was left with very little GABA, and likely a lot of glutamate. Therefore, he became violently tremulous.

How to Fix This: The best possible solution to this kind of predicament is to halt all GABA1a drugs while stimulating the other four GABA sites all at once. Not using any GABA1a drugs will allow the neurotransmitters at this site to up-regulate, coming to its own natural balance. Stimulating the other GABA sites will counteract his high glutamate, and make this detoxification as safe as possible. Moreover, decreasing the agitating glutamate with glutamate inhibitors like Zonegran will cause the balance between GABA and glutamate to shift in GABA's favor.

Treat Zonigran:
↑↑
↓↓

Zonigran increases GABA & Decreases glutamate
Doesn't Hit GABA 1a site

The GABA production needs to be increased at the other four GABA sites. To accomplish this, the GABA-like drug Robaxin, along with 10mg of the GABA drug baclofen three times a day, will be used. The drug BuSpar, a calming serotonin drug of the 5ht3 class, will possibly be used as well. He will also be given phenobarbital, a GABA drug, for just four to five days while his GABA1a sites up-regulate.

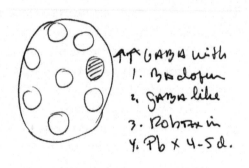

↑↑ GABA with
1. Baclofen
2. Gaba like
3. Robaxin
4. Pb x 4-5d.

The Result: After four days of treatment in the detoxification unit, this patient's panic attacks ceased, and he had no seizures, nor any cardiac events. He was calm, and the phenobarbital was discontinued. He will be discharged on Neurontin and Robaxin for several months, along with BuSpar and baclofen. Remember, when you leave the GABA1a site alone, it will up-regulate, and that person will slowly become calmer over weeks time, with a reversal and the brain finding its natural balance.

Case Study #13
Treating a Dopamine Deficiency

Patient Profile: A 31-year-old male habitually goes on a cocaine binge once every three months. He is married and a nonalcoholic. Normally he functions well working at a regular construction job, but then all of the sudden he gets what he describes as "tunnel vision." His family can sense when something is going wrong with him and for a week or two, he can only focus on cocaine until he finally succumbs to his cravings. The result is a consistent pattern of behavior: he leaves the house and sits in a motel room using high-dose cocaine usually for a three-week period.

As for his parents, his father has an alcoholic history and his mother, some sort of mood disorder. Though her mood disorder was never officially diagnosed, the patient described her mood as *unpredictable* his entire life, and a presumptive diagnosis of bipolar disease was made.

Diagnosis: To treat this man successfully and determine where the problem lies, we must look at the schematic of the

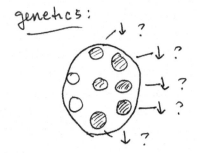

eight different neurochemical systems. Since alcoholism runs in his family, it is possible that up to six of his neurotransmitter systems are out of balance – GABA, serotonin, glutamate, endocannabinoid, opiate, and/or dopamine.

However, this man does not crave alcohol; he only craves cocaine. Being a dopaminergic drug, cocaine has an agonist effect on D2 and some D3, so he likely has some sort of dopamine imbalance. In the past, he used methamphetamine, which also has an ef-

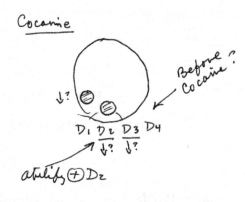

fect on dopamine, specifically D1 and D2. Dopamine imbalances are common bedfellows of mood disorders, one of which he likely inherited from his mother.

Treatment: This patient had been treated with Wellbutrin, having minimal success. Wellbutrin is a noradrenergic, dopamine, and acetylcholine stimulant medication, but clearly the dopamine in Wellbutrin was not sufficient to curtail his use and his relapses. The best bet now is to use a D2 dopaminergic drug such as Abilify to stop the cravings. We will increase his dosage until his cravings subside. Most articles advise only short-term use of Abilify, while others find long-term use to be beneficial. Therefore one must consider other adjunctive drugs such as naltrexone or tricyclic drugs, which activate both norepinephrine and dopamine.

There were a lot of variables involved in the approach to this patient's treatment. A chemical dependency program in any of the cases mentioned in this book is recommended. Recall that naltrexone inhibits dopamine from hitting the dopamine receptor sites, allowing these sites to then proliferate in response to not being hit. This allows the dopamine system to up-regulate and lets other dopamine regulatory effects become active and beneficial. The question now is how bupropion (Wellbutrin) works on D1 and D4; it is unknown at this time.

Case Study #14
The Unpredictable GABA1a Site

Patient Profile: A 32-year-old male has suffered from both obsessive–compulsive and general anxiety disorders for most of his life, but now has a new complaint. He just recently increased his prescription dosage of lorazepam (Ativan) to 12mg per day and since, has actually experienced an *increase* in agitation. His psychiatrist states that he cannot increase his dosage of the GABA1a-activating lorazepam drug any higher because it is no longer effective.

Consider: GABA and its five different types of receptor sites are located throughout the brain. This man was hitting the GABA1a sites with such concentrated frequency until they became so down-regulated, that there were few active receptors available for stimulation. Since GABA's calming effects are opposed by the agitating effects other neurotransmitter systems, namely glutamate, this decrease in GABA stimulation created an imbalance, resulting in more unopposed agitation.

What is occurring within this patient's brain is similar to that which occurs in the straining heart of an individual experiencing congestive heart failure. When the heart muscle is weak and cannot contract, the body tries to keep alive by producing excessive amounts of adrenaline (that is catecholamines) in an attempt to activate the heart to pump even harder. The catecholamines have receptor sites throughout the heart muscle. The over-stimulated catecholamine receptor sites slowly fade away and become inactive. The treatment method to combat this specific aspect of congestive heart failure is to use beta blockers, which block the catecholamines, allowing the receptor sites to up-regulate. This results in the sudden improvement of the heart muscle's strength and contractility. (Of course this is only one medication among many that is used to treat congestive heart failure.)

Likewise, what happens to a heart's catecholamine receptor sites during congestive heart failure is what is happening to this patient's GABA1a sites. By taking huge doses of GABA1a drugs, his GABA1a sites have faded until virtually none are functional. Instead of being calmed down by the lorazepam, his GABA sites were becoming disabled, causing him to become more and more agitated as the glutamate was no longer being counteracted by the proper amount of GABA.

Treatment: To treat this patient we will start by immediately discontinuing the 12mg of Ativan, and instead stimulate the other four GABA sites. The GABA1a site should then realize that it is no longer being hit, and thus return to a more stable level. The patient's own GABA system will take control of the GABA1a site over several weeks, and the patient will become calmer. To attain this goal, we will give the patient Neurontin, Robaxin, baclofen, and BuSpar, as well as phenobarbital (just for five days). These GABA drugs will load up the other sites as much as possible without toxicity.

Results: After the first day of treatment, he was no longer shaky; his hands were completely still. He had no diaphoresis, and his heart rate and vital signs were normal. All this progress despite going through withdrawal was attained by loading the other GABA sites and leaving the GABA1a site alone. It amazed the nurses that this patient was neither shaking nor tremulous within 24 to 36 hours of having no more lorazepam. The patient continued to be quite calm. Fluvoxamine, a medication used to treat obsessive-compulsive disorder was also prescribed.

Thinking Long-Term: Aside from the GABA1a site, the only other GABA site that we know to have an addictive response is that where phenobarbital activates the system. After the initial five days of detoxification, phenobarbital is no longer needed to combat the symptoms of withdrawal as long as the other three GABA sites continue to be activated. We like to save that phenobarbital site for any possible future detoxification and treatment the patient might need, and do not like to modulate or train that site to up-regulate.

When presented with a difficult detoxification case, keep in mind, *balance* is the key. By using your understanding of the neurochemical systems, as well as visualizing how the drugs activate the different systems, you can succeed at helping your patient to achieve a proper balance.

A Final Word

The brain and its neurotransmitters are incredibly dynamic. It has astonished me to learn and see every day in my practice just how interconnected these neurotransmitter systems are.

Whether you have read this book out of curiosity or necessity, it is my hope that you use your new found knowledge to better society, be it by assisting your patients more effectively or by helping a loved one to escape the entrapment of addiction. Please share what you have learned with anyone willing to listen. The knowledge within these pages has saved lives and will continue to do so on a larger scale only if you are willing to help.

Not only has this knowledge saved and improved lives, it has given hope to thousands in a way too personal to describe.

Genetic neurochemical imbalances are a real problem in our society, and they are more prevalent than ever previously acknowledged. These imbalances are the culprit behind countless cases of alcoholism, drug addiction, anxiety disorders, depression, and so much more. It is only by acknowledging the source of many of these problems, that we can offer practical solutions and continue the search for better ones.

For those with loved ones suffering from the pains of addiction,

I hope this book has helped. Everyone deserves to be informed. I hope this book has provided you with the understanding and confidence necessary to seek solutions, whether for your own neurochemical imbalance or assistance for a loved one. There is hope. Solutions are out there.

For doctors, nurses, and medical staff everywhere, I hope this book has equipped you with the knowledge necessary to better assist your chemically dependent patients to a life of lasting sobriety.

Best wishes to you all.

Dr. Fred Von Stieff
December 2011
www.braininbalancebook.com

CPSIA information can be obtained
at www.ICGtesting.com
Printed in the USA
LVOW04s0828040117
519694LV00015B/163/P